MORE TALES FROM A LONG ROOM

Peter Tinniswood was born in Liverpool. He is the author of *Tales From A Long Room* and six highly praised novels including *A Touch of Daniel*, *The Stirk of Stirk* and *Mog*. He has also written extensively for television and his credits include the classic BBC comedy series *I Didn't Know You Cared*.

He is currently working on a new series for Central Television entitled *The Home Front*.

MORE TALES
FROM A
LONG ROOM

Peter
Tinniswood

ARROW BOOKS

Arrow Books Limited
17–21 Conway Street, London W1P 6JD

An imprint of the Hutchinson Publishing Group

London Melbourne Sydney Auckland
Johannesburg and agencies throughout
the world

First published 1982

© Peter Tinniswood 1982

This book is sold subject to the condition that it shall
not, by way of trade or otherwise, be lent, resold,
hired out, or otherwise circulated without the pub-
lisher's prior consent in any form of binding or cover
other than that in which it is published and without a
similar condition including this condition being im-
posed on the subsequent purchaser

Set in Linotron Sabon
by Rowland Phototypesetting Ltd
Bury St Edmunds, Suffolk

Made and printed in Great Britain
by Hazell, Watson & Viney Ltd
Aylesbury, Bucks

ISBN 0 09 928800 1

For Mr Winston Place
of Lancashire and England
and Mr Robin Bailey
of Nottinghamshire

Contents

Contents

1

Witney Scrotum

It is a fact well known to all lovers of our dear 'summer game' that the inhabitants of cities and large conurbations north of a line drawn from the Bristol Channel to the Wash are without exception shiftless louts with weak chins and smokers' coughs, mean-lipped wives and slack-jawed children, all of whom, regardless of their place of birth, speak with Birmingham accents and eat with their mouths open.

I am not a prejudiced man.

I am prepared most readily to except from these strictures the city of Sheffield, whose inhabitants deserve the special sympathy of the whole nation.

On their behalf candles should be lit, church bells

rung, high masses celebrated by His Holiness George Pope the First and public fastings made on beds of cricket boot spikes by those two eminent gurus of the game, Swami Rumsey and the Krishna Milburn.

And why?

Because these fine, upstanding people with their distinctive blunt thumbs and concave shin bones are the victims of the greatest act of vandalism perpetrated in this country during the last five centuries.

I refer, of course, to the dissolution, the desecration and the sacking of one of Britain's holiest and most revered of ancient shrines – the cricket pavilion at Bramall Lane.

I am not a prejudiced man, but the scum responsible for the execution of this monstrous wickedness deserve the ultimate punishment known to civilized society – a day's incarceration in the Trent Bridge radio commentary box with Mr Tony Lewis and Mr Trevor Bailey.

Why do I state these opinions so unequivocally?

Old age, dear readers, old age.

As a body grows older and the juices run thinner and bleak winter gardens show fewer and fewer signs of approaching spring and desire withers in the nether regions of the popping crease, so do subtle changes take place within the mind.

In my case, for example (as in the case of many others of my acquaintance), I find that I now consider that everyone under the age of forty, man, woman, child and beast alike, looks exactly like Mr H. D. 'Dicky' Bird.

Indeed in moments of the darkest despair I feel that everyone over the age of forty, man, woman, child and beast alike, looks exactly like Mr H. D. 'Dicky' Bird.

Can you imagine the ghastliness induced by this state of mind?

Think of its implications.

The Miss World Championship is won by Mr H. D. 'Dicky' Bird.

Our own dear and precious Miss Una Stubbs looks like Mr H. D. 'Dicky' Bird.

So do Miss Lionel Blair, the Chief Rabbi, the Queen of the Belgians and the lady from the village dog biscuit shop.

Dear God, even Ching Ching, the panda, looks like Mr H. D. 'Dicky' Bird – small wonder, therefore, that successful mating did not take place with Mr N. Nanan of Trinidad and Nottinghamshire.

Under these circumstances I console myself more and more with my bottles of Brown and Robertson vintage tawny port, my half-scale Meccano models of Mr K. D. 'Slasher' MacKay and the knowledge that one at least of Britain's most noble institutions is still prospering.

I refer, of course, to the English village.

Here, thriving in all their rampant glory, are some of the finest flowerings of the English way of life – foul language, dirty wellingtons, wife-swapping and after hours drinking.

Since that emaciated vileness, Tinniswood, wrote about me in a recent book, for which incidentally he paid me not one single penny, I have been inundated with requests to give more detailed information about my place of domicile.

I have always been most reluctant to do this.

However, recent events, which I shall presently relate, have forced upon me 'a change of heart'.

So with a certain amount of trepidation and in the spirit of those immortal words of that most celebrated master of the English language, Mr E. R. 'Elizabeth Regina' Dexter – 'here goes'.

The village of Witney Scrotum lies 'somewhere in England'.

I shall not identify its geographical location more precisely for fear of its being invaded by fleets of motor charabancs stuffed full of grinning Nips, square-headed Huns and foul-smelling Frogs with unshaven armpits.

I am not a prejudiced man, but I firmly believe that scum of this sort should be shot on sight or interned behind barbed wire for life on bread and water together with the hordes of lilac-haired, pre-pubescent, stoop-shouldered yobboes from nearby Keating New Town with their boils and their pimples and their filthy under-clothes and work-shy parents driving Japanese cars the shape of over-sized pilchard tins and wasting the natural resources of our precious planet by gobbling up vast acres of forest land to provide paper on which to print the cricket reports of Mr Tony Lewis.

Where was I?

Ah yes – the village.

Suffice it to say that our village nestles in a gentle curve of that most exquisite of chalk streams, the Somerset Kitchen, sheltered from the harsh northerly gales by the rolling uplands of the Mendis Hills.

All around are rich woodlands of hanging oak, beech and chestnut and on the exposed escarpments grow the two varieties of rowan, athol and eric.

Lush water meadows leading to the coppice at Cowdrey's Bottom are the haunt of winter wildfowl –

red-crested tolchard, lindwall, wellard and common pridgeon.

Mother Nature's munificence is indeed boundless.

Every prospect pleases.

And, looking down on our village, totally dominating it from every angle, is the massive and magnificent bulk of the ancient earthwork of Botham's Gut, and carved into its chalk flanks are the badges of every single first class cricket county cut by dissident Yorkshire professionals imprisoned during the long and bitter Wars of the Sellars.

I have given a general picture of Witney Scrotum.

Now let us fill in the details.

By far the finest way to approach the village is by the old carters' route from Milton Abbas and Milton Arthur.

We cross the River Kitchen by the old stone packhorse bridge at Dredge's Elbow, and as we turn the corner by the old artesian Popplewells we find ourselves on the outskirts of the village of Witney Scrotum.

Pause awhile.

Do you see those low stone buildings to your left?

Once they were the home of the ancient gimblett and tremlett makers, but now, alas, with the disappearance of the old rural festivals of Toad-Skinning Thursday and Circumcision Saturday, there is no longer a need for their craft and only one of their breed now remains.

And he, poor chap, lives in somewhat reduced circumstances in Bournemouth eking out a precarious living with his circumciser's bradawl behind the ladies' heel bar at Marshall and Pocock's department store.

But let us wipe away our salty tears and continue our stroll through the village.

Above us the rooks caw hoarsely in the elms for all the world like a massed choir of Robin Jackmans appealing for lbw at Sabina Park.

On the roof of the golf ball museum we see a pied wagtail flicking its tail and bobbing its head, constantly fidgeting, forever twitching, an avian Derek Randall, looking down into the yard of Fearnley's Mill, where the village senior citizens are happily working in the gentle sunlight on the latest batch of thatched space invader machines.

Move on, dear reader, move on.

Tread softly past the wrought iron gates of Squire Brearley's Queen Anne mansion, for we do not wish to disturb that gentle, kindly old scholar as he works on the eleventh volume of his masterpiece, 'A Treatise on the Surrey Philosophers, Hobbs and Lock, including an Analysis of their Influence on the Leg Spin Theory of the Middlesex and England philosopher, J. A. Jung, with particular reference to Lord Eric Russell's *A History of Western Philosophy* and its Impact on Wittgenstein's analysis of the laws of cricket entitled "A battle against the bewitchment of our intelligence by means of language".'

A soft word and friendly greeting to our lovable and harmless village idiot, old Ben Stansgate, and here we are in the centre of Witney Scrotum.

Do you see?

There facing each other across the square are those twin bastions of village life, the pub and the church.

Look.

Sitting on a bench outside the Baxter Arms supping scrumpy and linseed oil shandies and drowsing in the sunshine are the venerable village elders Messrs Arlott, Mosey, Frindall and Alston, endlessly yarning about old campaigns in India, Australia, South Africa and the deathless, arid prose plains of British South West Dexterland.

They raise their forelocks to us as we leave them to their dreams and cross the square to the church.

What an exquisite Saxon edifice.

Clean and pure of line like a cover drive by Peter May.

Sturdy and honest like an over bowled by David Brown.

Chaste and virginal like an anecdote told by Barry Wood.

And inside the church displayed in a place of honour by the statuette of St Kevin de Keegan, the patron saint of endorsements, is one of our village's most cherished possessions.

It is, of course, a relic of the Blessed St Tony Greig of the Sorrows – a fragment of his money belt torn from his person during the Exodus From Sussex and lovingly restored by the master craftsman, Sebastian Coe, for a fee of £97,000, that being the cost of his second-class train fare from Sheffield.

Let us walk through the churchyard with its gravestones standing splintered and askew, its brooding yews and its monument to those brave village lads who fell in battle over countless centuries with its simple and moving inscription: 'Died of Drink'.

Let us rest our arms on the old moss-covered stone wall and gaze in peace and tranquillity at the pride and joy of Witney Scrotum – its cricket ground.

There stands the pavilion, timbered and hunched.

There stands the scorebox, tarpaulined and hushed.

There stands the groundsman, sullen and sloshed.

But wait.

Look at the pitch.

Dear God, it is scarred and criss-crossed with mounds of newly dug earth.

Have vandals been at work?

Have extremists carved into the turf of the wicket those dreaded words:

'Robin Marlar Is Innocent OK.'

No, my friends, that is not the case.

Relax, and I shall now relate my tale.

It starts in the early days of the present season when a small ridge appeared in the pitch just short of a length at the hoof warehouse end.

As the weeks progressed so did the ridge increase in size.

The members of our team, and, indeed our opponents, too, were content to accept it as one of the many natural hazards which add such spice and excitement to our beloved 'summer game' – exploding tea urns, infected egg and cress sandwiches, lady wives with loathsome unmarried sisters in Cheltenham and confounded Bedlington terriers constantly scratching and flecking and burying apostle teaspoons in the commodore's herbaceous border.

I am not a prejudiced man, but . . .

Where was I?

Ah yes, the ridge.

It was our village blacksmith, Gooch, who discovered

the true nature of the protruberance, and thus earned for himself a place of honour in cricket's 'hall of fame'.

He was batting against our visitors, a Michael Parkinson Invitation XI, which curiously enough included neither David Niven nor Billy Connolly, when a fastish away swinger delivered by their opening bowler, Mr Sammy Kahn, father of the former Pakistani Test cricketer, Majid, struck the ridge and, flying upwards and inwards, struck him a fearful blow on the left temple.

In a rage Gooch, normally the mildest of men, thrashed out with his bat at the offending ridge.

Soon turf and earth were flying in every direction.

And then of a sudden there was a loud metallic clank.

Gooch stopped dead in his tracks.

He knelt down and produced from the depths of the crater he had made with his bat a battered, rusting metal cask.

Our stumper, the village sub-post master and accredited poacher, Prodger, took out from his hip pocket the oyster knife he habitually used for prising open the registered letters addressed to old Grannie Swanton, and, grinding his dentures most fearsomely, unlocked the cask.

An amazing sight met our eyes.

There glinting in the bottom of the cask were six small irregular-shaped metal objects.

What were they?

Were they Mr Barry Wood's missing front teeth?

No.

It was old Squire Brearley, who with a stroke of pure genius, guessed their true identity.

'They are primitive Iron Age coins,' he said.

'And there are six of them. Six? Don't you realize the significance of this?'

We shook our heads.

Squire Brearley tugged his grizzled, shag pile beard and smiled.

'It is obvious,' he said.

'Six coins.

'Who uses six coins?

'Of course, my friends, of course.

'They are the coins used by some ancient umpire to count the number of balls bowled in some ancient over during some ancient and hitherto unknown cricketing culture.'

We gasped with admiration.

We threw up our hats in the air.

Strong men wept.

Poor old doddery Mosey spilled a jug of prime Cliff and Bradley Lancashire Exhibition bitter down the front of his moleskin romper suit.

Dear Lord, we had made history.

When news of our discovery reached 'headquarters', the duty flying squad detachment from MCC's stand-by archaeologists' unit was instantly dispatched to our ground to commence a 'dig'.

Hence, dear readers, the scars on the pitch.

Hence the mounds of earth.

Hence the unrestrained jubilation in our village, for here at Witney Scrotum we had discovered a previously unknown primitive culture to rank alongside those of the Beaker People, the Windmill Hill Folk and the Wombwell Cricket Lovers' Society.

And what treasures were brought up from the bowels of the earth.

Let me list just a few:

Two fossilized score card printing presses and a pair of stumper's gloves made from flint.

The earliest known biography of Sir Geoffrey Boycott.

Ornate bronze brooches bearing mottoes such as 'Botham Is King' and 'Tony Lewis for Grandstand'.

An early pottery pavilion gents urinal stall still blocked by the original filter tip cigarette butts.

Jockstraps made from a primitive form of tupperware and sellotape, thus proving, what had long been suspected, that even in those distant times men were in possession of what we now know as 'private parts'.

We know little of the lives of these people.

From remains of food examined in a charnel pit we can deduce that even during the Iron Age cricketers were eating potted meat sandwiches and angels on horseback.

From motifs on their pottery artefacts we know that, as now takes place with losing Australian Test captains, human sacrifice was resorted to in times of crisis.

But the most important discovery concerned their method of burial, and from this is derived their name in the archaeological canon.

It was towards the end of the dig that a long barrow was discovered in the region of deep third man just short of the groundsman's underground whisky still.

When it was painstakingly and carefully uncovered, there were revealed rows and rows of human skeletons laid out feet first in individual leather containers with primitive handles on either side.

And thus they are now known to scholars as the Cricket Bag People.

Speaking for myself entirely personally, there is only one thing which marred the pleasure of this discovery.

When the skulls of these people were taken to London and scientists set to work on them to reconstruct their facial appearance, it was revealed that every one of them without a single exception looked exactly like one man and one man alone.

Yes, dear readers, you have guessed.

It was Mr H. D. 'Dicky' Bird.

I am not a prejudiced man, but. . .

2

The Boys of Summer

The winter sun filters shyly through the shrouds of mist that hush the water meadows by Cowdrey's Bottom.

The wing beat of swan, the yackle of woodpecker, the scrawk of gull, the crunch of wellington boots on new-dropped snow – I am at ease, dear readers.

The lady wife lies confined to her bed with bedsock poisoning.

I am content.

Her loathsome unmarried sister is safely snowed up in Cheltenham.

I am at peace with the world.

What did the poet say?

Clear the air!
Clean the sky!
Wash the wind!
Take stone from stone and wash them.

Bloody fool.

None the less, it confirms what I have always stead-fastly maintained throughout all the many vicissitudes which life has thrown in my way – monsoons in the Bay of Bengal, typhoons in Tahiti, confounded Bedlington terriers snapping at one's ankles en route to the ablutions offices in the bleak watches of the night.

My belief is this:

The association between men of letters and practitioners of the 'summer game' has been long and felicitous and has enriched and ennobled every strand in the weft and the warp of our way of life.

The poet I have just quoted, for example, is Mr T. S. Eliot.

And he, of course, achieved even wider fame as the brother of the Derbyshire cricketer and Test umpire, Charlie.

Indeed, as I pen these lines, there are playing currently in the first class game several of our most distinguished 'literary lions'.

I think of Gloucestershire's Brian Brain, author of *Room at the Top*, of Denis Amiss and his hilarious rib-tickler, *Lucky Jim*, of Yorkshire's David Bairstow and his moving and sensitive *A Kind of Loving*, and, of course, the delicious Mr P. 'Beryl' Bainbridge of Gloucestershire, author of *The Bottle Factory Outing*, the mirthquaking account of the annual waysgoose of the Professional Cricketers' Association.

In addition to these celebrated novelists we find playing for Northamptonshire the distinguished poet and philosopher, Wayne Larkins, while Lancashire are lucky enough to have on their staff that amusing and witty *Guardian* cartoonist, Jack 'Posy' Simmons.

Incidentally is it not somehow comforting and appropriate that the current 'skippers' of the 1981 England rugby union football and cricket teams are named respectively Beaumont and Fletcher?

I await in a fever of excitement for the day when the captains of our national ladies netball and rugby league sides are named respectively Sherrin and Brahms.

However, it is not all 'one-way' traffic.

The literary history of the western world is full of examples of highly esteemed writers plying their craft on subjects dear to our beloved 'summer game'.

I think immediately in this context of Samuel Beckett, author of the controversial and deeply influential, *Waiting for Boycott*.

But how many of you, dear readers, know of two equally stimulating masterpieces which come from the pen of this well-loved 'Broth of a Boy'?

Grossly neglected, I feel, is his surrealistic novel about a long, damp and wicketless afternoon in the life of an Australian fast bowler playing for Lancashire, entitled *Malone Dies*.

And I can recommend without reservation the same author's brilliant playlet about the final years in the career of a Gloucestershire and England batsman, entitled *Crapp's Last Tape*.

Another writer who has ventured into the 'genre' is

Mr Len Deighton, better known perhaps as the author of a series of dazzlingly witty and inventive spy novels.

Without hesitation I would bestow the sobriquet 'a minor masterpiece' on *Bomber*, his biography of the Gloucestershire and Nottinghamshire spinner, Mr B. D. Wells.

Although Mr Deighton would, I am sure, be the first to pay tribute to the 'inside knowledge' of the subject he received from his father, the former Lancashire and Army cricketer, Captain J. H. G. Deighton.

Let us venture further into our examination of the subject.

The list of writers is indeed extensive.

It includes, among many others:

Thomas Armstrong and his biography of an extremely small Lancashire batsman, *Pilling Always Pays*.

Captain W. E. Johns, creator of the immortal Biggles, and his superb adventure yarns, *Gimblett Mops Up* and *Worrell Scores A Ton*.

Edna O'Brien's finely-constructed chronicle of family life in successive generations of an Essex county team, *The Casualties of Pearce*.

I much admire Evelyn Waugh's savagely satirical bowlers' coaching manual entitled *Put Out More Faggs*, and his affectionate monograph on Mr Robin Marlar, *The Loved One*.

The moving television screen has also provided a masterpiece in Mr Jeremy Sandford's tear-jerker set on the practice ground at Headingley and called *Athey Come Home*.

And the world of classic literature has produced a colossus in the shape of Mr D. H. 'Sid' Lawrence's epic story of a Surrey fast bowler, entitled *Sons and Govers*.

Dear Lord above, even the Americans have got into the act.

Who can ever forget Ernest Hemingway's masterly account of Mr Ian Botham's hitting exploits in the recent Test series against Australia, *Across the River and into the Trees*, and his sensitive and generous tribute on the retirement from the first-class game of Kent's most distinguished wicket keeper/batsman, entitled *A Farewell to Ames*.

You may wonder, dear readers, from whence I have acquired this extensive knowledge.

Well, literature has been a life-long interest of mine, along with cigarette cards, train-spotting, indoor yodelling, amateur fretwork, vintage Vimto, ancient bannisters and the incidence of litotes in the collected works of Lord Henry Blofield.

Indeed in my study now lying under the supine body of the cat are several priceless manuscripts which their famous authors have hitherto refused to publish.

Let us cuff the cat round the ear, and, giving him a thorough thrashing with a six-inch ruler, remove the manuscripts and examine them more closely.

This one, for example:

An extract of a play written by Mr Harold Pinter, brother of the former Burnley and England centre forward, Ray.

It is entitled *The Umpire*.

ACT ONE: SCENE ONE

A CRICKET GROUND. A MATCH IS TAKING PLACE. IT IS A MINOR COUNTIES MATCH. IT IS

BETWEEN KENT SECONDS AND HERTFORD-
SHIRE. A BATSMAN WALKS SLOWLY TO THE
WICKET. THE UMPIRE AT THE BOWLER'S END
WATCHES HIM SILENTLY AS HE PLACES HIS BAT
CAREFULLY INTO THE CREASE AND SLOWLY
RAISES TWO FINGERS.

BATSMAN: Middle and leg.

[PAUSE]

UMPIRE: I shouldn't be standing at Sidcup.

[PAUSE]

I should be standing at Lords.

[PAUSE]

I got my papers at Lords.
If only the weather would break, I'd be able to get
to Lords.

[PAUSE]

What did you say?
BATSMAN: Middle and leg.

[PAUSE]

UMPIRE: You see, what it is, you see, I changed my
name.
Years ago.
I been going around under an assumed name.
D. O. Oslear's not my real name.
No.
Not by any stretch of the imagination

[PAUSE]

Were you wanting something?
BATSMAN: Middle and leg.

[PAUSE]

UMPIRE: Spencer.
  Tom Spencer.
  That's my name.
  That's the name I'm known by, anyway, when I'm
    standing at Sidcup.

                                      [PAUSE]

  When I'm standing at Maidstone it's Aspinall.
  Ron Aspinall.

                                        [PAUSE]

  Nice name, Ron.

                                        [PAUSE]

  What was it you were wanting?
BATSMAN: Middle and leg.
UMPIRE: It's the shoes, you see.
  I can't go to Lords in these shoes.
  Last time I went to Lords in these shoes I seen the
    President, name of Brown.
  F. R. Brown.
  I said, you haven't got a pair of shoes, have you? I
    heard you got a stock of shoes here, I said.
  'Piss off,' he said.

                                        [PAUSE]

  You were saying?
BATSMAN: Middle and leg.

                                        [PAUSE]

UMPIRE: Piss off.

In that extract the part of the umpire was played by
Miss Constant Cummings.
  The batsman was played by Dame Derek Evans of
Glamorgan.

The identity of the author of the next manuscript to be examined might surprise some lovers of the 'summer game'.

She is none other than Miss Barbara Cartland who in recent years has achieved national fame for her appearances on the moving television screen, bellowing in stentorian tones:

'Sit!'

However, there is another side to this talented creature.

Her deep, innate modesty and intense shyness have tended to obscure the fact that she is a writer of no little distinction in the field of romantic fiction.

Her novels, written with intense artistic integrity and awesome fastidious diligence to the minutest detail of character, plot and dialogue at the rate of one every two hours, have brought her a small but loyal following among retired colonels of the Royal Army Dental Corps, middle-aged shop assistants on the bacon counter of Tesco's Foodstores and fast bowlers confined to the ablutions offices during MCC tours to India and Ceylon.

It is high time her works reached a wider audience and with this end in view I am happy to present an extract from her enchanting novelette, *Bowling the Maiden Over*.

She stood there on the greensward at Brighton.

Brighton! Here the regency bucks and dandies had conducted their dalliances with the fashionable courtesans of high society.

Brighton! Here the bright young things of the twenties had come for passionate weekends of chaste romance under a sickle moon with the gentle waft of scented sea breezes whispering to them the poetry of love.

Brighton! Would they ever really establish themselves in the First Division of the Football League?

Her reveries were interrupted as a ripple of applause rippled among the spectators whose honest ruddy faces rippled the splintered summer sunlight.

She looked up and her heart missed a beat.

It was him.

No.

It was he.

He strode out to the wicket with that lissom lilt to the limbs, that purposeful manly tread, that ripple of rippling muscles that turned her knees to jelly.

And how her heart fluttered to the jut of his jaw, the straightness of that aristocratic aquiline nose, the haughty glint to those broodingly passionate smouldering eyes that rippled beneath the rippling black of his noble mane.

'Dexter, Dexter,' she breathed to herself.

Now she could feel the juices quicken in her body as he approached the wicket.

Nearer and nearer and nearer he came and then of a sudden he was standing next to her.

In person.

What would he say if he knew that it was her – no, it was she – who was standing at the bowler's end disguised as the celebrated umpire and mobile hat stand, Mr H. D. 'Dicky' Bird?

She was soon to have the answer.

Flexing his arms and rippling the muscles of his jaw he turned to her and said:

'Whatho, Dicky. How are the old piles this morning?'

At that moment something in her snapped.

The floodgates burst open and torrents of passion engulfed

her soul and in a blind ecstasy of rippling sensuousness she flung herself at her beloved bringing him crashing to earth just short of a length at the batsman's end.

'Dexter, Dexter,' she cried as she smothered his face with a passionate ripple of kisses and tore with feverish fingers at his cravat and his Gunn and Moore waterproof boil plasters.

'What the devil are you doing, Bird?' bellowed the manly rippling voice of the precious being around who – no, around whom – her whole existence revolved.

'I love you, I love you,' she gasped.

'Oh, God,' he said, 'it's Arthur Jepson all over again.'

Thus it was three weeks later she found herself at Lords sitting in front of the disciplinary committee composed of some of the highest dignitaries in the 'summer game'.

But the words they spoke made only a rippling drone in the back of her fevered mind.

She had eyes for only one man.

He sat facing her, slowly munching a Bounty Bar.

Their eyes met, and she felt a ripple of animal passion pass between them.

Oh, the sensuous lilt to his lips. Oh, the proud and noble tilt to his head. Oh, the ripples of passion in his eyes.

'Bedser, Bedser,' she whispered to herself.

Finally I have a task of honour to perform.

Duty compels me to put right one of the greatest acts of calumny ever perpetrated against our greatest poet of the 'summer game'.

I refer, of course, to Mr Dylan Thomas, known throughout the world as 'Wales's answer to Mr Wynford Vaughan Thomas'.

I have before me the manuscript of his majestic poem, 'I see the boys of summer in their ruin.'

It is this work which has been the object of such vileness.

There are certain long-haired, damp-fingered nancy boys with scent-laden armpits, who, posing as critics and arbiters of public taste, claim that the subject matter of this poem is what Lord Baden-Powell called in a moment of genius 'beastliness'.

Could anything be more damaging to a man's reputation than an accusation of such baseness?

Viler still, could anything be more designed to cast dark shadows on the characters of the countless millions of virtuous, virginal young men who have played our dear 'summer game'?

Let us look at the first verse of this superb poem and scotch forever this wicked accusation.

> I see the boys of summer in their ruin
> Lay the gold tithings barren
> Setting no store by harvest, freeze the soils;
> There in their heat the winter floods.
> Of frozen loves they fetch their girls,
> And drown the cargoed apples in their tides.

Good God, the meaning is clear enough.

It is this:

'The boys of summer' are those honest, hard-working, journeymen county cricketers, who, knowing they have no chance of making the MCC winter touring party, go out in the last match of the season to have a damn good joyous slog 'setting no store by harvest' of a decent score and looking forward to a winter spent with lady wives and sweethearts quaffing vast quantities of cider by drowning 'the cargoed apples in their tides'.

Could anything be plainer than that, dear readers?

These pomaded, simpering, limp-wristed homos with their disgusting sexual proclivities – how dare they impute that the flower of our cricketing manhood with their long, slim fingers entwining rich and silky balls and their firm fresh hands sliding slowly up and down quivering erect bat handles could ever have been guilty of 'beastliness'?

I rest my case.

3

Batman

The summer of '81.

What a vintage season.

What deeds of derring-do.

Such excitements, such tensions, such dramas.

It will live forever in the memories of all lovers of our blessed 'summer game'.

In Witney Scrotum, too, we had 'our moments'.

The white admirals returned to my garden for the first time in fifteen years.

The auxiliary fire brigade was called out three times to deal with conflagrations in the copse at Cowdrey's Bottom.

And, most blissful of all, for seven solid weeks the lady wife's confounded Bedlington terriers were laid low with a bout of canine piles.

But these, of course, are the musings of a 'village Hampden'.

Enough of nonentities.

Let us concentrate on that one man who strode through the season like a colossus, who thrilled us, who inspired us, who made strong men weep tears of joy, who sent surges of long-lost patriotic fervour coursing through the veins of every man, woman and child in this dear country of ours, who excited the immortal Mr E. R. 'Elizabeth Regina' Dexter to dizzy heights of sublime prose, which even he in his eminence could scarcely have hoped to attain.

I quote:

'He played a real "snorter" of an innings.'

Such command of language.

Such beauty of style.

And to whom was he referring?

Of course, dear readers, of course.

He was referring to that most celebrated son of Botham City – Batman.

There now – the secret is out.

I was sworn to secrecy, I confess, but after sleepless nights of torment and torture wrestling with my conscience, I have reached the conclusion that it is my duty, despite prior reassurances, to reveal the truth, the whole truth and nothing but the truth to the nation at large.

So – to use another of Mr E. R. 'Elizabeth Regina' Dexter's memorable phrases – 'here goes'.

Botham City, the home town of our hero of the

summer of '81, is more widely known to you and me, dear readers, as Keating New Town.

Keating New Town – what a sad, dismal testimony to all that is base and vile in contemporary society.

It was built with such high hopes.

Yes, it was a noble ideal to provide a new town in the heart of the English countryside for the poor wretches from the slums of our loathsome industrial cities.

But dear God, was it necessary to build the bloody thing a mere spit and a Honda ride away from Witney Scrotum?

The execrable selfishness of town planners, architects, local councillors, members of Parliament and similar scum is totally beyond comprehension.

There are times on summer Sunday evenings when it seems that the whole of Witney Scrotum is under siege by moronic louts riding oversized electric razors, picking their revolting ape-like noses with nicotine-stained fingers the size and shape of frost-bitten parsnips, and all of whom appear to be called Wayne or Darren.

I am not a prejudiced man, but when I think of rabble of this sort using up the precious oxygen of this dear planet of ours to fill up their soot-clinkered lungs in order to give them the strength to suck on their limp home-rolled cigarettes and to ceaselessly and publicly scratch their private parts, around which the whole of their nauseating existences revolve, I am filled with . . .

No, dear readers, no.

I shall contain myself.

I shall concentrate my attentions on 'the hero of the hour' – Batman of Botham City.

Let me conduct you to his place of abode.

Come with me to Keating New Town, and let us search out our hero 'in situ'.

We stand for a moment in the main square of the town, the Grand Place Hetherington, situated on the site of the ancient Grauniad Abbey.

The Grand Place Hetherington – what a pathetic hulk it now is.

Unemployment, vandalism and simple 'bad planning' have reduced this once proud public monument to a broken-down shambles.

Boarded up now are the grog shops, the wine bars, the taverns, the pubs, the open-air cafés, which gave it such gaiety and animation in the days of its prime.

It stands now eerie and deserted, bewildered and defeated by the brutal hands of fate.

Let us wipe away our tears and, turning our backs on this old ruin, hurry away down Billington Avenue.

Here, too we are faced with desolation and despair.

What folly to have expected the sub-human louts from the loathsome industrial cities with their luminous socks and their bulbous wristwatches to respond to the cultural offerings of the Harris-tweeded, limp bow-tied weirdos and nancy boys from the Arts Council and the St John Stevas Academy of Woodcraft and Rock Climbing.

Just look.

The Dame Sybil Thornber Memorial Theatre is an empty shell.

The De Jongh Theatre of the Absurd is a rotting hulk, cruelly defaced by graffiti, most of it in the handwriting of Brian Chugg, L. P. Samuels and Enid J. Wilson.

And, saddest of all, the building which housed the Jill

Tweedie Feminist Consort Fully Committed Parabolic Circus is now used as a mail order warehouse for the sale of novelty condoms, Polly Toynbee naughty flannelette nighties and Katie Stewart erotic cricket pads.

We carry on down Billington Avenue, and shortly we arrive at the Peter Jenkins Industrial Estate.

What a wasteland of unfulfilled promise and thwarted expectations.

Do we blame the planners once more?

In this case I think not.

Who could possibly have forecast all those years ago that there would be such a dramatic and catastrophic collapse in the British stapling machine industry?

Who could have predicted the world-wide slump in demand for bakelite shoe horns and non-stick underpants?

Who could have foreseen the havoc the Japanese would play among our traditional export markets in odourless fly-paper, tungsten pumice stone holders and musical bulldog clips?

Now the factories which housed these enterprises lie still and silent, and over all of Keating New Town there hangs the ghastly spectre of unemployment, poverty and the television reviews of Miss Nancy Banks-Smith.

Let us hurry away, for now we are within reach of our hero.

Turn the corner into Lacey Close.

Cut through the snicket into Rodda Drive and there in front of us is his place of residence.

Here is the shrine to which cricket lovers from all over the country will soon come to worship, if I reveal its identity.

Shall I?

Shall I, shall I?

Yes.

Yes, I owe it to you, dear readers.

The abode of Batman of Botham City, the hero of the summer of '81, is a corner shop.

And above the window written in letters of lime green and modest size is the legend:

'Neville Gribley — Wavy Line Grocer.'

I hear the gasps of horror.

The shock waves reverberate from every part of the country and shake my priceless collection of miniature cricket balls here in my study at Witney Scrotum.

Batman a grocer?

The man who single-handedly won two Test Matches for England against Australia is a purveyor of baked beans, Meltonian shoe polish and special offer toilet rolls?

Yes, 'tis so, dear readers, 'tis so.

Press your nose against the window of the shop and look inside.

Yes.

There he is.

That man in the nigger brown cardigan, the baggy chalk-stripe flannels and the grease-scuffed Hush Puppies reaching up for a packet of sultanas is indeed Batman.

Now do you understand?

It is only in moments of greatest national emergency that he rips off his Aertex singlet, his clip-on St Michael bow tie and surgical sandals and dons the uniform of Batman — the pristine white sweater under which bulges the noble barrel chest, the snow-white flannels under which ripple those whipcord muscles, the navy-blue war helmet and the false beard from the Alec and Eric Bedser Tee Hee Joke Shop.

At all other times Batman is simple Neville Gribley, five foot three in his stocking feet, seven and a half stone (excluding the three ball point pens and seven propelling pencils he carries constantly on his person) and a man of profound meekness, sensitivity and modesty.

The 'real' Batman, the 'real' hero of the summer of '81, is a simple soul frightened of mice and cockatiels, totally opposed to strong drink and bold women, a devotee of 'Crossroads' and the works of O. S. Nock, a man whose principal pleasure is indoor embroidery and the restoration of vintage bicycle pumps.

Let us enter the shop.

The bell jingles merrily.

We listen to his soft and diffident voice as he speaks to his customers.

'Yes, Mrs Gower, we do have a special offer in hair nets this week. Very reasonable, and if you buy six, you get a free oven pad.'

'Hello, Mrs Fletcher, love. You're looking down in the dumps again. Why don't you try the gregory powder this week instead of the Ex-Lax?'

'Morning, Mr Gatting. No we don't stock those. I'd try the barber, if I was you.'

Let us creep past him and enter his private quarters.

How neat. How tidy. How fastidious.

In his diner/kitchenette everything is spotless.

The tupperware gleams. The teatowels are starched snowy white. The muslin covers on the marmalade jars are immaculate. And there is not a single stain on his tin of Bournvita.

And upstairs in his dear little bedroom with its Clara Cluck frieze his night attire is neatly folded in his Mike Brearley autograph pyjama case, there is not a speck of wax in his nightlight holder and his Hobbs and Sutcliffe Teamaker stands proudly on his cane bedside table next to the silver-framed photo of Mr Ian Chappell.

And there under the window is a low bookcase.

Let us examine the books it contains, for these can reveal much about a man's nature.

There they are, still in their original dust jackets – the complete works of Catherine Cookson, a first edition of *Bunkle Buts In*, seven *Radio Fun* albums, three *Teddy Tail* annuals, seven volumes of Arthur Mee's guide to the counties of England and a paperback anthology of the best of the cricket reports of Mr Tony Lewis.

But, of course, it is 'the smallest room in the house' which is most indicative of his character.

How delicately he has embroidered his toilet roll covers.

How assiduously he has hoovered the drip mat and harpicked the bidet.

The whole establishment smells like a timid early morning glade in the heart of the New Forest, and far be it from me to destroy that pristine freshness after our lunch of lobster vindaloo, tarka dhal and home-brewed curried lager.

Let us descend the stairs and talk to our hero, for it is his evening break, and he is only too happy to share with us his pot of Mazawattee tea and his plate of custard creams.

Let us allow him to 'speak for himself', shall we?

'Yes,' he says, as with crooked little finger he delicately dunks a biscuit in his willow pattern tea cup. 'Yes, I have got ambitions.

'My fondest ambition, i.e. what I'd like to do most in this world, is to own a knitting wool shop in Basingstoke.

'Or failing that I'd like to go half shares in a garden centre, concentrating mainly on the indoor pot plants.

'I seem to have an affinity with them. You should see my Busy Lizzy.'

Is he happy with his lot?

'Oh yes. Yes, indeed. You see, there's a lot to recommend this life.

'I think I'm providing what I call "a service to the community", which is not provided by the supermarkets with their impersonal service and their relative inaccessibility.

'And I do think I compete with them most favourably as regards prices, particularly on my bacon counter where I do a very good line in knuckles.

'You see, the nice thing about this job is that you become what I like to call "a member of the community".

'For instance, I'm always ready to break off serving to have a chat and a natter with one of my "young mums" or help my senior citizens over the road if they're "unsteady on their pins".

'The things I hear sometimes. Honestly!'

And what about his social life?

'Well, basically, I am a rather shy and reticent person once out of the environs of the shop.

'I used to like going to the cinema until they started showing rude films.

'And I used to go every Friday to the public baths until they converted it to mixed bathing.

'Basically, though, I'm what I like to call "a home-loving person".

'I like watching "Crossroads" on the telly – isn't it scandalous what they did to Meg Richardson? – and I have to confess I'm rather fond of "Blankety Blank", particularly when they have Kenny Everett on it. Isn't he a yell?

'I like "Give Us a Clue", too, although I do wish Michael Aspel would tell us sooner when they're going to put the clue up on the screen.

'In the main, however, I prefer what I like to call "the wireless".

'I like Ken Ford on "Gardeners' Question Time" – hasn't he got a deep manly voice? – and I'm a great fan of Louise Botting on "The Money Programme".

'Also I like "Yesterday in Parliament", the Legal Beagle on the Jimmy Young Show and any programme that deals with our "feathered friends".'

And what about romance?

Is there a little lady in his life?

'Oh no.

'You see, basically, I'm very shy as regards what I like to call "the opposite you-know-what".

'As I never drink anything stronger than Vimto, I never go to public houses, and that's where you meet young ladies these days, isn't it?

'Mind you, I do dream about them sometimes.

'I have this dream which I have quite often actually.

'There's these young ladies and they're wearing nothing but cricket caps and they're heaving and straining and pulling the heavy roller at Taunton and they're being whipped by Vivian Richards who's wearing nothing but a gold lamé jock strap and they've painted his nipples carmine and his buttocks are. . .'

At this moment there is a strident buzz on the telephone.

It glows, and it pulsates.

Our hero leaps up from his uncut moquette Waring and Gillow granny rocker and wrenches up the receiver.

'Yes, yes, yes,' he says tersely.

He slams down the receiver.

Gerrow.

Zak.

Yoweee.

Tcheroooooooooooooooooo.

In an instant he is transformed into Batman.

The chest bulges.

The muscles ripple.

He raises his bat to his shoulder.

He adjusts his abdominal protector.

And:

Gerrow.

Zak.

Yoweee.

Tcheroooooooooooooooooo.

In a screech of tyres and a deep-bellied snarl of jet engine he disappears from our view in his blood red Bothamobile.

Yes, Batman is off again to do battle for Queen and country.

Whither is he bound?

To knock the stuffing out of Indian spin bowlers?

To thrash the living daylights out of Mr H. D. 'Dicky' Bird?

To liberate Afghanistan from its Russian overlords and free Tibet from the yoke of Chinese oppression?

Maybe.

It is, however, my personal hope that he is off to Westminster to give a severe ear-cuffing to that slimy little shit, Mr Leo Brittan.

However, all in good time we shall know the purpose of his mission.

Let us leave now.

One moment.

The lady wife sent me on an errand for a packet of marzipan paste.

There it is on the shelf next to the tins of pilchards and the packets of bi-carb.

No, dear readers, I have not forgotten.

I have left the money on the counter.

Dear God, we don't want a visit from Batman in Witney Scrotum.

4

Five Non-Cricketers

It is a fact totally beyond dispute that one of the greatest and noblest joys of summer for men of 'cricketing bent' is that wondrous and precious moment when the lady wife scoops up her confounded Bedlington terriers and encamps for Cheltenham to spend three weeks with her loathsome unmarried sister.

Peace and serenity.

The lady wife is gone, and the sun shines stronger in the heavens, the birds sing sweeter in the meadows, the whisky glows tangier in the decanters, and a chap can go to bed secure in the knowledge that his nocturnal ~~ablutions~~ activities will not be irretrievably soured each time he returns to the bedroom by his lady wife barking in that hideous hectoring voice:

'I hope you've shaken your Thing properly.'

Dear readers, is there any greater joy known to man than the slow pad-padding through the rooms of a house shorn of the odious omniscient presence of its mistress?

The very fabric of the building seems to croon with contentment.

The dust gathers softly on the bookshelves like dandruff on the collar of a Surrey blazer, shreds of burning tobacco float gently down to the china rug like the acrid smuts of Leeds floating down to the wicket at Headingley, and the cooker top grows greasier and greasier for all the world like the hair of the young Denis Compton.

There are moments to savour.

For now a man may indulge in those forbidden pleasures of the flesh, which so outrage the cruder sensibilities of the lady wife.

How perfect to stand at the open french windows of the drawing room on a fresh summer's morn and, by carefully extending the right leg sideway and raising the right foot three inches above the ground, slowly and rapturously break wind.

How sublime to abandon all furtiveness and with blithe abandon affix to the corner of the kitchen tablecloth the contents of one's left nostril.

How blissful to lie pink and soaking in a brimming bath with carnal thoughts of Mr K. D. 'Slasher' MacKay flickering through the mind, knowing that one's reverie will not be shattered rudely by the lady wife marching in with her hateful dipstick and declaring:

'You brute, there's more than three inches of hot water in this bath.'

It was with pleasurable anticipations such as these suffusing my whole being in a deep and rosy glow that I sped homewards in the trusty Lanchester after depositing the lady wife and her confounded Bedlington terriers with her nauseous pile of consanguinity at Cheltenham.

I knew of an inn where strong ale was dispensed in mellow old pewter tankards.

I knew of a wayside cottage where thick and sizzling gammon was served with orange-yoked eggs and plump, sizzling mushrooms, golden potato cakes and mugs of sweet brown tea.

I knew of a riverside hostelry whose landlord had once opened the batting for Minor Counties versus Pakistani Eaglets and whose scrumpy was the colour and consistency of Tony Cordle's bathwater.

And then it happened.

A sudden howling and screeching, a volley of staccato explosions for all the world like Mr Robin Jackman appealing for a catch behind the wicket at Port of Spain, and the infernal engine of the trusty Lanchester went dead.

In vain did I thrash the brute.

In vain did I curse it.

The beast stood silent and still at the side of the road, its chrome radiator grill sneering superciliously at me, like the hideous elongated smile on the face of the Chappell brothers.

I lashed out with the toe of my boot, and as I recoiled backwards, howling with pain, I caught a glimpse of a figure standing placidly at a garden gate.

Those features were familiar.

So was the dress – the Pierre Cardin crocodile skin smoking jacket, the cerise suede knickerbockers, the Russell and Hobbs electric doeskin sneakers.

Yes, it was Woodcock of *The Times*.

Dear old Bruce Woodcock – a friendly face in hostile climes, a broad shoulder to cry on, a certain provider of strong liquor and scrumptious victuals.

I was not disappointed.

He took me gently by the arm and led me inside his charming old house, the Curacy, named thus in honour of the Rev. J. K. Aitchison of Scotland and the present Archbishop of Canterbury, Dr Fred Rumsey.

And there as the evening shadows lengthened and herons returned to their roosts high in the shimmering elms we ate packet after packet of his home-made bilberry-flavoured crisps and quaffed glass after glass of his home-brewed jock strap wine.

How he yarned about old times – those epic scraps of his in the ring with Tami Mauriello and Lee Oma and those later epic scraps in the press box at Taunton with Mr Robin Marlar and his musical father, Gustav, as the assembled hacks struggled for possession of the single Bill Frindall patent portable scorer's commode.

Later still as he passed round his home-stilled Thermogene gin he showed me a selection of some of his most prized possessions.

Item after item was dropped to the floor or trampled underfoot as we took it in turns to lurch to the 'facilities' behind the Fay Weldon autographed sightscreen at the bottom of the garden.

By the time we cracked the seventh bottle of home-cured bunion ointment whisky I confess we were both slightly 'stinko', not to say totally obfuscated and hiccius-doccius.

Nonetheless when he withdrew from the deepest recesses of his 'treasure chest' the pride of his cricketing souvenirs and mementoes my senses were of an instant sharp and crystal clear.

It is not generally known, I suspect, that Bruce Woodcock, apart from being chief cricket correspondent and men's fashion editor of *The Times*, is also editor of *Wisden's Cricketers' Almanack*.

It is even less well known that while that august journal publishes annually its five cricketers of the year, it also has specially written, although not for publication, its five non-cricketers of the year.

It was a selection of these articles which dear old Bruce offered for my perusal.

I know he will not object to my sharing a few with you, dear readers, as at the moment I purloined them he was lying prostrate on the floor drinking large draughts of home-made lint juleep out of an extremely rare example of Dame Peter West's left dancing pump.

So here for your delectation are five Wisden Non Cricketers of the Year:

The Maharajah of Rutnagur

Rutnagur achieved distinction as being the fattest man ever to play first-class cricket.

In his prime he weighed in at 52 stone and was forced to play the majority of his innings seated in a reinforced pre-stressed concrete howdah.

In a memorable innings of 8 made in eleven hours while playing for Delhi against Madras Nude Bicyclists

Gymkhana he came to the wicket weighing 33 stone and when finally given out weighed 37 stone, this being the result of his having consumed during his occupation of the crease five prawn vindaloo, eight chicken dhansak with fried rice, eleven mutton tikka with bindi bhajee, two trunkfuls of spiced poppadoms, one plate of curried abdominal protector in cricket bag sauce and both the umpires.

He was forced to retire from the first-class game when, with his side requiring only one run to defeat Bengal State Vegetarian Laundries and Dry Cleaners and thus win the Ranji Trophy, his massive bulk stuck fast in the pavilion door on his way to the wicket and, despite the heroic efforts of seventeen bull elephants on heat to drag him clear remained firmly embedded in the structure of the building, thus enabling his opponents to claim victory as no other batsman of his side was able to reach the wicket.

He was finally released through a joint operation involving a platoon of Ghurka sappers, a battalion of the North West Frontier Mounted Artillery and a squadron of dive bombers from the Royal Indian Air Force.

Next day his body was stuffed with 65 tons of bombay duck and pilaw rice and is now used as the spare heavy roller on the ground of the Bombay Mutual Tango and Gentleman's Onanists Club.

Banks-Smith, 'Nancy'
The only woman ever to have kept wicket for Worcestershire.

Many judges are of the opinion that she could ultimately have represented her country, but for one crucial failing in her armoury – a relentless desire to be funny at all costs.

Selection committees were prepared to ignore the ugly, crab-like stance when batting and the staccato, stuttering, disorientated style when 'wearing the gloves'.

What they could not ignore was her lack of generosity to team-mate and opponent alike through her refusal to cease dispensing jokes of profound feebleness.

Died laughing at her own jokes during an episode of *Brideshead Revisited*.

Currently employed on the staff of the *Guardian*.

Yarwood, M. J. K.
'Mike', as he is universally known to friend and foe alike, achieved a 'bumper' year in the season 1980.

As J. A. Ormrod of Worcestershire he came twentieth in the first-class batting averages.

And as P. J. Hacker of Nottinghamshire he reached twelfth position in the national bowling averages.

He also umpired the Second Test match against Australia in the persons of D. O. Oslear (the well-known cricketing misprint) and Mr H. D. 'Dicky' Bird.

Stansgate Wedgwood-Benn, Anthony
Without any doubt 'Gaters' was the outstanding schoolboy and varsity cricketer of his generation.

An aristocrat among batsmen, a crown prince among bowlers, a fielder of peerless elegance, he towered like a golden-skinned Colossus above his contemporaries.

He was a true all-rounder in the noble traditions of

Fry, Studd and Spooner, for not only was he a natural sportsman, excelling at assocation football, high hurdles, Graeco-Roman wrestling, crown green bowls and three card brag, but he was also an oustanding scholar, winning at his school the Michael Foot gold medal for casuistry and engine spotting seven years running.

But it is as a cricketer that he achieved his most memorable successes.

Few who were present will forget the brilliance of the treble century he scored before lunch while playing for his school against a formidable TUC Young Professionals XI skippered by the astute and wily Clive 'Roly' Jenkins.

Witnesses still talk with bated breath of the deviousness of the spinners he sent down while taking all ten wickets against a Socialist Dissidents and Thespians XI featuring Judith Hart and Gerald Kaufman playing the front end and back end respectively of Mr Denis Healey.

A glittering future of rampant success seemed assured.

What went wrong?

Some say it was overweening ambition, a desire to captain England 'at all costs'.

In the opinion of this writer, however, this is totally false, for 'Gaters' was a natural leader and the honour he so desired would have come inevitably to him regardless of any special endeavours on his part.

No, this writer steadfastly maintains that the failure of 'Gaters' to achieve the highest of honours and successes could be put down to one simple fact – an unhealthy and totally destructive pre-occupation with the 'low life'.

If only he had stuck to 'his own kind'.

When he came down from the varsity, he had the whole world at his feet.

Surrey, Middlesex, Kent and Sussex clamoured for his services as skipper.

With his natural beauty and grace, his wit, his erudition, his aristocratic birthright, he could have 'had his pick' and made his mark in any sphere of human activity he cared to choose.

But what did he do?

He turned his back on the first class game.

He abandoned his family seat in the country and his stately town house in London, he threw away his doeskin jodphurs and his shantung MCC blazers and, donning flat cap, muffler and moleskin waistcoat, began playing league cricket in the north of England.

Why?

Some people say it was because he gained a vicarious excitement from associating with people so obviously inferior to him in every facet of life.

Some people maintain he fell under the malign influence of the seedy, balding Yorkshire professional, Scargill, who used him simply as a means of obtaining free elocution lessons.

Others claim that it was the inherent nobility and generosity and passion of his nature that drove him on a missionary crusade to the dourlands of the north to preach to the working classes his fervent belief that the cover drive, the late cut and the wristy leg glance were not the sole province of the upper classes.

But whatever his motives poor 'Gaters' never fitted in.

Try as he might (and his endeavours were indeed assiduous) he never mastered the behaviour patterns of his new-found colleagues in northern league cricket.

The slack jaw, the gormless glaze to the eyes, the mean slit to the mouth, the swift drag on a Park Drive dimp between overs 'stumped' him completely, and, being a naturally gifted fielder, he found it impossible to drop his aitches.

Within a few years the gaiety and abandon of his stroke play had been replaced by a dour forward prod.

The lissom grace of his fielding had been replaced by a stoop-shouldered plod on the boundary and a weary underarm lob to the keeper.

The bowling arm dropped lower and lower.

He was just 'going through the motions'.

Eventually in a moment of supreme humiliation he was dropped from the team and relegated to the humble duties of baggage master and scorer.

Poor 'Gaters'.

His tragedy was that he desperately wanted to be a 'Player', but breeding and background doomed him to be forever a 'Gentleman'.

Tinniswood, Peter
The ultimate non-cricketer.

Holder of the record Lancashire opening partnership of 567 with his partner, Winston Place.

5
Sibson

Like all lovers of our dear 'summer game' I am addicted
to Taverner's fruit drops.

Thank God, I had the foresight to lay down sufficient
quantities of the great vintage of 1956.

Now, sucking a particularly majestic green fruit drop
(as always the finest of the vintage) I find my mind filling
up with overpowering remembrances of times past.

And I grieve.

I grieve for the loss of those institutions, those people,
those objects of everyday life, which gave this great
country of ours its infinite superiority over the mass
rabbles of non-cricket-playing dagos, wops, frogs,
Huns and similar scum too ghastly to mention.

There are grave questions to be asked about our past, dear readers.

Whatever became of Felix Mendelssohn and his Hawaian Serenaders?

Where oh where are Kitty Bluett and Pearl Hackney?

Why the demise of plus fours, nosebags, tram conductors' mittens and Lancashire leg spinners?

Will there ever be another Fred Loads?

I confess without shame that as the years draw in on me inexorably with the bleak relentlessness of a Michael Parkinson interview, it is nostalgia which warms my old bones and lags my thin veins against the icy chills of contemporary life.

Admit it, dear readers, it is thus with you.

It is nostalgia, pure and simple, which keeps you sane in these hideous days of Colonel Swanton's Fried Kentucky Chicken, H. D. 'Dicky' Bird and his loathsome instant custard, Jimmy Hill, Nigel Smarmer-Stiff, Tony Gubba Row and his brother, Ramon, Reichsmarschal von Pickering and Feldwebel Vine, the Dowager Duchess of Took, Pamela Stevenson (how much better the world would have been had he stuck to wicket keeping with Hampshire) that vileness Tariq Ali, and his father, the umpire Bill, Dennis Lillee.

Dennis Lillee – dear Lord above!

Only this morning I read in my newspaper that this wretched man took up his stance at the wicket with a bat which contained in its splice a digital clock.

Digital clocks – dear Lord above!

To my untutored eyes it seems that everything we purchase these days contains a digital clock.

Where will it all end?

Shall we have the beastly contraptions on our jock-straps, our bicycle clips, our MCC membership cards, our. . .

But no. Let me calm myself.

Let me comfort myself in the secure and tender embrace of blessed nostalgia.

As I sit now in the fluff-bound study of my home in Witney Scrotum I see all around me the souvenirs of my past.

My beloved grandfather's death mask, the nostrils of which serve as most useful receptacles for my pipe cleaners and hedgehog reamer.

My even more beloved grandmother's yak-hide ear trumpet which terrorized so many of the literary eminences of the time who attended her celebrated 'salons' at her London residence, the Aspels.

It is reliably reported in the memoirs of Dame Peter West that my grandmother used this ferocious instrument to great effect during a violent and physical argument between the author of *Vanity Fair*, Harry Makepeace Thackeray, and Mrs Gaskell, author of the definitive biography of a beloved Lancashire cricket captain, *Cranston*.

But I own, it is the souvenirs of my late father which move me most.

There on the table next to my Uncle Fishlock's drip-dry polo sticks I have them laid out in a place of honour.

I particularly treasure three sets of his best drinking braces made from toughest Michelin tyre tread and special non-corrosive metal buckles, his magnetic hip flask, his indoor whisky still disguised as a bust of Charlie Smirke, and his portable kidney douche.

Dear, dear father; he it was who many many years ago instilled into me feelings for the theatre which I hold to this very day.

How can I describe those feelings?

How can I do justice to the loathing, the nausea and disgust I hold for the whole panoply of conceit, vainglory and arrogance supported by unseemly hordes of braggarts, self-publicists and pomaded pansies?

I except from these strictures, of course, the celebrated light comedian and chanteuse, Mr John Inman, brother of that fine Pakistani Test cricketer, Mr Inman Khan.

And that doyen of the English stage, Sir Alf Richardson, husband of the former proprietress of 'Crossroads', Meg, and father of the two cricketing brothers, Peter and Derek.

But back to my father and his abiding interest in all matters of a Thespian nature.

Apart from being Chief Inspector of Bicycles and Tandems to the East Bengal Mounted Customs and Excise Hussars my father also achieved considerable distinction as an amateur inventor.

He it was who invented the inflatable toothpick for the use of lifeboatmen.

He it was who invented the luminous arch support for the use of explorers during the perpetual darkness of the arctic winter – a device also used by opening batsmen during the perpetual darkness of Old Trafford Test Matches.

It was in his capacity as an inventor that my father first met that giant of the English stage, that female colossus, who charmed us, enchanted us and captured our hearts for more than six generations until she was 'put down' by humane killer in the outside toilets of the Garrick Club.

I refer, of course, to Mrs Chester Dromgoole.

Her beauty was unrivalled.

Her wit was unparagoned.

How well I remember seeing her as a young boy in that ripping farce, *Arsenal and Old Lace*.

Among the dazzling cast was the bewitching Miss Winifred Emery, mother of that most subtle and sensitive of English actors, Mr Dick Emery, who coined as a catchphrase a remark made by Sir Donald Bradman to Mr Harold Larwood during the infamous 'bodyline' series in Australia:

'Oooh, you are awful, but I like you.'

It was a few weeks after this theatrical event that my father was summoned to a weekend house party at the country residence of Mrs Chester Dromgoole to demonstrate to her his latest invention, the portable wig.

Mrs Dromgoole, always a fitness fanatic, had recently been playing the arduous part of Othello in Shakespeare's play of a very similar name.

In order to achieve maximum physical soundness she had taken to training with members of the Millwall Association Football Club.

Unfortunately the constant heading of a sodden football had caused an unsightly bald patch to appear on the crown of her pate, thus necessitating the intervention of my father and his latest cranial creation.

Mrs Dromgoole expressed herself delighted with the wig, which served the dual purpose of concealing her trichopathic deficiencies and providing a warm and comforting night bed for her beloved Boston terrier, named after Julius Caesar, who coined another of cricket's immortal catchphrases:

'Come two, Brute.'

My father never ceased to talk with affection and enthusiasm of the blissful four days he spent at the gracious stately home set in the heart of the green and rolling hills of rural England.

Dear old 'Weskers' – how right that it should now be one of our country's most treasured national monuments.

The company that weekend was dazzling.

Statesmen, diplomats, politicians, great soldiers, dukes and duchesses, BBC executives and their wives strolled along the gravelled paths, lingered in the sweet-smelling conservatories and gossiped on the fine-cropped lawns.

Over breakfast that first morning my father shared a table with those two eminent men of letters, Sir Sacha Distel, and his brother, Dame Edith.

Later on the same day my father played a game of shuttlecock and battledore against a certain Irishman by the name of Wilde, who was partnered by a typically oily, garlic-stinking Frenchman, name of Proust.

My father was partnered by Lord Kitchener.

The sodomites won.

The perfect weekend was marred for my father by only one thing – the presence of a Norwegian playwright, who had achieved a certain modest success in his own country as the author of the play *Piers Gynt*.

His name was, I believe, Sibson.

Sibson's gloomy mien, his dark brooding silences and

the shapeless, shabby raincoat he wore constantly despite the noble, blazing English sun cast a sullen blight on the company which was not to be assuaged despite Mrs Dromgoole's heroic efforts to entertain her guests with her far-famed impersonations of the Langridge brothers, James and John.

My father well remembered his first encounter with Sibson, who was seated at an exquisite rosewood and tupelo escritoire next to the sightscreens in the writing room.

'Whatho, Sibson,' said my father. 'Scribblin' again, eh?'

Sibson fixed my father with a pair of cold blue eyes and said:

'Sir, I am writing a play in which the heroine refuses to discover herself, and her conflicts and her tragedy are the results of this refusal.

'Longing for life and yet afraid of it, she refuses to admit this fear and convert the energy of her conflict into action.

'And so at the centre if the play will be a mind turning upon itself in a kind of vacuum.'

'I see,' said my father. 'And are you using washable ink in your fountain pen?'

Many years later my father saw this play, *Edna Gobbler* in the company of two of the most august members of the cricketing establishment, Mr H. D. G. Leveson-Gower and Sir Pelham 'Plum' Warner, creator among many other things of the immortal catchphrase:

'Mind my bike.'

During the second act Sir Pelham, who had found increasing difficulty accommodating his nether regions, clad as they were in cricket pads and abdominal protector, in the narrow confines of the orchestra stalls, said in a very loud voice:

'Who are all these bloody Norwegians anyway?'

'Sir,' said my father. 'One is a puisne judge. The other is a scholar engaged in the history of civilization. And the chap with the big nose is his wife.'

'Splendid pair of shoulders on her,' said Leveson-Gower. 'Wonder if she'd like to open the bowling for me at the next Scarborough Festival?'

And with that the gentle snores of two of the most distinguished administrators in the history of the 'summer game' echoed sweetly round the theatre.

They were disturbed only when some damn fool let off a pistol at the end of the play, thus causing Sir Pelham to spill half a box of orange-flavoured chocolate dragees down the front of his MCC blazer.

I mention this incident only to emphasize a point that has so often been overlooked by the so-called experts and self-appointed arbiters of public taste, with their vile socks and adenoidal snufflings – the overriding influence exercised by the game of cricket on the most momentous and significant movements in the history of the drama.

For example, it was during that weekend at the residence of Mrs Chester Dromgoole that Sibson conceived the central theme of his most famous play.

A lot of bosh and tommy rot has been spoken and written about this, and I intend to 'put the record straight' here and now.

The facts are these:

On the Sunday afternoon, as was customary at these

house parties, Mrs Dromgoole split her guests into two teams to take part in a game of cricket.

Sibson was nowhere to be found.

It was the obsequious, shifty-faced butler, Billington, who finally discovered him skulking in the attic dressed in shabby greatcoat, woollen gloves and a dirty, reddish-brown wig, thus bearing a marked resemblance to Mr Patrick Moore in his Sunday best.

On being summoned to Mrs Dromgoole's presence and informed of her desire that he take part in the cricket match, Sibson thew up his hands and cried:

'But, merciful God, one doesn't do that kind of thing.'

It took all the tact of my father's hostess to persuade him to don Free Foresters' cap and I Zingari sweater, although he jibbed at wearing cricket flannels, protesting:

'One should never put on one's best trousers to go out to battle for freedom and truth.'

On seeing him take a net with Dame Flora Hobson, and her sister, the eminent drama critic and unicyclist, Dame Harold, my father well understood Sibson's reluctance 'to chance his arm'.

For his aptitude for the game could be summed up in three well-chosen words:

'No bally good.'

The two teams were captained respectively by Field Marshall Hindenberg and Lady Violet Bonham-Carter, a noted 'purveyor' in her own right of top spinner and chinaman.

Sibson opened the batting for Lady Violet's side and with typical Scandinavian two-eyed stance faced the first ball delivered by the immortal Lord 'Rolf' Harris.

The noble Lord, bowling over the wicket, sent down a short-pitched ball which rose sharply from the pitch and struck Sibson flush in the groin.

Much was the merriment of the spectators as the melancholic father of all subsequent plays concerned with the inner experience of the individual and the assessment and revaluation of his past at some ultimate turning point of his soul's pilgrimage hopped round on one leg clutching his private parts.

When he had regained his breath, Sibson pointed feebly at Lord Harris and cried:

'Go round, Peer.'

This Lord Harris did, and, bowling round the wicket, struck Sibson a formidable blow on the right temple.

It was obvious by now to one and all that his Lordship was determined to humble and humiliate the Norwegian for the gloom and despondency he had caused to settle on the company in the previous days.

The third ball thudded most frightfully into Sibson's chest.

The fourth, a beamer, caused him to fling himself full length on the pitch.

The fifth knocked out his two front teeth and the sixth, the most perfect of yorkers, totally wrecked his castle beyond redemption.

Sibson had not troubled the scorer.

And as he stormed back to the pavilion swinging his bat angrily, muttering dark Scandinavian curses and grinding his remaining Nordic teeth, we realize now only too well the origin of his most celebrated of plays.

I refer, of course, to *The Wild Duck*.

Later he was to write a somewhat less distinguished

play about the family of a former Lancashire and England opening batsman, entitled *The Pullars of the Community*.

6
The Royal Wedding

Like all lovers of our beloved 'summer game' I found last year's Royal Wedding the most damnable and thundering nuisance.

It confirmed conclusively what I have always believed most fervently and passionately.

It is this:

Any sphere of human activity given the 'seal of approval' by the distaff side in the person of the lady wife and all the other long-haired, loud-voiced, hairy-legged fraternity with their things on the front of their chests and their twanging corsets and their rasping knickers and their confounded Bedlington terriers and their loathsome unmarried sisters in Cheltenham can only be regarded by civilized man and member of MCC alike as utterly vile and detestable.

Consider those enterprises which receive their approbation — hanky-panky, dusting, armpit-shaving, hectoring, setting mousetraps, wiping lavatory seats, cutting toenails, lighting fires, chopping wood, repairing greenhouse guttering, changing the plugs on the trusty Lanchester and, worst of all by far, going to weddings.

Dear Lord, it would not be so bad if they did not insist on their menfolk being present and taking an interest while they are indulging in these squalid and totally unnatural undertakings.

Even after all these years I still feel a deep and brooding resentment towards the lady wife who insisted on my being present at our wedding, despite my having warned her six months previously that on that very day I had a long-standing arrangement to attend the annual luncheon of our cricket touring club, the Ditherers, at the Dexter Arms, Langridge-on-Sea.

I told her I was prepared to compromise.

I made a firm promise that if I could spare the time from the Scarborough Cricket Week, I would make every endeavour to spend a few days in her company on our honeymoon.

But no.

She 'dug in her heels' and with typical female selfishness insisted on my making a personal appearance at our wedding in tickety-boo order, despite my presenting her with a doctor's note to the effect that I had a deep-seated allergy to spats.

In this context I am reminded of a dear friend of mine

talking in bleak and gloomy tones about the arrival of yet another of his detestable offsprings.

'Were you present at its birth?' inquired a mutual acquaintance and 'more than adequate' stumper.

'Good God, no,' replied my friend. 'It was bad enough being present at its conception.'

This observation represents precisely my feelings on being compelled through the medium of the moving television screen to be present at the Royal Wedding.

Ghastly.

Horrendous.

Yet how differently the morning had started.

There was not the slightest hint of the vileness that was to follow.

There was joy and optimism in the air.

The sunlight glinted and sparkled on spider's web and dragonfly's wing.

Chiffchaffs sang. Swifts screeched.

Cocks crowed.

Cows lowed in the pastures below the massive earth-work of Botham's Gut.

The lady wife snored heavily in the conjugal container for all the world like a simmering tank locomotive at rest in some drowsy country branch-line siding.

I stepped carefully over the pink and twitching bellies of the slumbering Bedlington terriers.

Pausing only for a swift and successful foray on the bowel movement front, I padded softly downstairs and breakfasted alone on the terrace.

The spotted flycatcher flittered in the wistaria.

Swallows swooped low to scoop the dew from the lawn.

Through the open upstairs window I heard the creak of springs as the lady wife turned over in the bed of Procrustes, sounding for all the world like a rusty tramp steamer shifting at her moorings in some silted Flemish creek.

What bliss lay ahead.

A slow potter in the garden, an hour's brisk indoor pig-sticking with my neighbour, the commodore, and then snorters in his summer house, swapping cigarette cards, comparing train-spotters' notebooks and softly yawning the afternoon away – could a man ask for anything more perfect?

I sighed with deep contentment.

I scratched long and lingeringly all those dark and secret orifices forbidden to man by countless generations of lady wives and stern-chinned mamas.

I crept up behind the cat and shouted in its ear.

When the brute turned round, I flapped my arms and jumped up and down and it fled, ears flat on its head, into the gooseberry bushes.

It's the only way to treat them.

I sighed once more with satisfaction and began my inspection of the garden.

How beautiful it looked.

The clematis jackmanii was in full bloom, the fruits swelled proudly on the Coxon's orange pippins, the Eric Russell lupins stood out from the herbaceous alan border erect and rampant, the bernard hedges were clipped neat and tidy, the berries of the berberis don wilsonae sparkled and above all towered the noble stand of the cypress Maurice Leylandi.

My reveries were rudely interrupted by a stentorian

bellow from the french windows.

The lady wife!

Oh God, had I forgotten to flush the toilet again?

No.

She bellowed once more.

'It's already started. It's on the television.'

My heart missed a beat.

My blood froze in the veins.

Chill fingers of fear rilled down my spine.

Had I got it all wrong?

Had I made the most colossal boo-boo?

With a trembling voice, cracked with panic, I said:

'But I thought the Test match was next week.'

Instantly there appeared on the lady wife's brow dark and clustering furrows like the coal black isobars on a weather forecaster's chart, denoting impending storms in Portland Bill and Peter Wight, and imminent gales in Biscay and Fred Astaire.

'It's the Royal Wedding,' she hissed through those familiar threatening yellow equine teeth. 'And I want you inside. This instant.'

I am no coward, dear readers.

I have faced the bullets of Pathan, the sabres of Uhlan, the spears of fuzzy wuzzy, the poisoned darts of pygmy, the records of Barry Manilow and the cricket reports of Mr Tony Lewis, and I have not flinched.

But at that moment I knew the meaning of fear.

Real fear.

I knew how the novice jockey felt approaching Becher's Brook.

I knew how Keith Fletcher felt awaiting the umpire's decision at Delhi.

I knew how Rimsky felt the night before he married Korsakov.

And I gave in.

Abjectly I surrendered.

With bowed head and hunched shoulders I slunk across the lawn like Mr Ian Chappell returning to the pavilion after a heavily disputed clean-bowled decision had gone against him.

Cravenly I entered the drawing room and slumped into my armchair opposite the moving television screen.

I had to.

There was no other way.

I simply could not risk being 'gated' for the week of the Scarborough Festival.

There was nothing to do but watch the moving television screen and 'grin and bear it'.

Dear Lord above, what a palaver.

What a fuss.

Goodness knows how much the wallahs at the BBC spent on setting it up.

The procession alone must have cost them a small fortune.

Rank after rank of horses and on their backs rank after rank of silly asses wearing brass coal scuttles on their heads.

Open carriages jam-packed full of grinning, waving boobies with long necks and damp chins.

No wonder, we are having to pay more for our licences and sit through endless repeats of 'Terry and June'.

Sheer, wanton extravagance.

The money would have been better spent buying

decent shirts for the weather forecasters and investing in a new set of dentures for Mr Phil Drabble.

There was one moment of pleasure in the wretched business, I confess, when the bride alighted from her carriage outside the church.

How wonderful for our dear 'summer game', I felt, that one of the most loyal and honest of county cricketers, Mr Terry Spencer of Leicestershire, should have his daughter Diana thus elevated to the ranks of royalty.

Once inside the church, however, gloom descended again.

The porcine snufflings of the lady wife mingled with the frightful racket of the organ played, I suppose, as usual by Mr Robinson Cleaver, and the ghastly screechings of the bugles played by, what seemed to me, members of the band of Dr Crock and his Crackpots.

I looked around at the congregation.

Dear God, never in all my life had I seen such a collection of big ears.

And the faces!

Black faces, yellow faces, Muslim faces, Hindu faces, pock-marked faces, shifty faces, leering faces – it was like looking at a team photograph of Warwickshire County Cricket Club.

On and on and on droned the service.

Up and down bobbed the congregation like spectators behind the bowler's arm in the pavilion at the Oval.

Never have I felt such misery and despair.

And then?

And then of a sudden I felt my senses sharpening.

My muscles tensed. The adrenalin began to pump. The nerve ends tingled.

Something about the ceremony was 'not quite right'.

What was it?

What the devil was it?

Had they forgotten to invite Cliff Richard?

No.

There he was in the fifth row next to the Beverley Sisters and Mr Winston Place and wearing a natty green ostrich feather hat.

So what in the name of blitheration was it?

Realization dawned in a sudden blinding flash, when a creature purporting to be Mr George Thomas, Speaker of the House of Commons, rose to its feet to deliver the address.

Of course.

It wasn't George Thomas.

It was Mr Tony Lewis.

I could recognize those obsequious, snivelling, adenoidal Welsh cadences anywhere.

And what was he doing there?

No, it was not the usual reason – he was not auditioning for another crack at 'Grandstand'.

He was there for the same reason as everyone was there.

He was a stand-in.

It all fitted into place.

Because of the security problems, the authorities had trundled out a vast cast of extras to take the place of the genuine participants and guests.

Think back, dear readers.

Think back, I beg you.

Who was the Archbishop of Canterbury?

Think, think, think.

Of course, it was Mr E. W. 'Gloria' Swanton.

And who was Princess Margaret?

Dennis Lillee.

Without any effort at all I can reel off a list of dozens of stand-ins.

Princess Anne – David Gower.

Captain Mark Phillips – Keith Fletcher.

King Olav of Norway – Bill Alley.

Nancy Reagan – Dame Peter West.

Prince Charles – C. H. Dredge.

The King of Tonga – Fred Rumsey.

Page boy – Mr David Constant.

Her Majesty the Queen – Mr E. R. 'Elizabeth Regina' Dexter.

The Duke and Duchess of Kent, Mr Angus Ogilvie, the high commissioners for Canada, Australia and New Zealand, Garter King of Arms, Princess Alice of Athlone, the Queen of Denmark, Prince Edward, Prince Andrew, the ambassadors of Burma, Finland and Costa Rica, representatives of the Womens' Institute, the Girl Guides Association and the Post Office Advisory Committee – Mr Ian Botham.

And these suspicions were confirmed when some chap claiming to be Miss Kerria Chihuahua stood up and catawauled so loudly at the top of his voice that the confounded Bedlington terriers fled screaming to the utility room.

And who was it?

Of course, it was none other than Mr Joel Garner of Somerset and the West Indies, and he was wearing a silly frock.

The pleasure that suffused my whole being at this

discovery turned swiftly to euphoria.

It was not only the Royal Wedding which was all pretence.

So was the whole of life.

Consider Sir Geoffrey Howe, for example.

Think of that boring voice, those torpid eyes, the slow and sluggish clanking of the brain, the endless plodding of the intellect – he's the reincarnation of an innings by Trevor Bailey.

And who is playing the part of Willie Whitelaw?

Think, dear readers, think.

Of course – it's Frank Keating.

The list continues:

Sir Keith Joseph – Lance Gibbs.

Norman Tebbitt – Mr H. D. 'Dicky' Bird.

Dennis Healey – Clyde Walcott.

Rhodes Boyson – Sir Geoffrey Boycott.

Mrs Thatcher – Mr K. D. 'Slasher' MacKay of Queensland and Australia.

Michael Foot – Derek Randall.

Roy Hattersley, Cyril Smith, Andrew Faulds, Dame Judith Hart, Black Rod, Lord Hailsham, Edward du Cann, Edward du Cann't, Dafydd Wrigley-Spearmint, Dame Eric Heffer, Miss Gerald Kaufman, Mr Joan Lestor, the Rev Ian Parsley, the 1922 Committee, the Tribune Group, 'Diddy' Willie Hamilton, Mr Winsome Churchill, Doctor Gerard 'Frankie' Vaughn, Anthony Wedgwood-Benn, Tony Wedgwood, Anthony Benn, Tony Wedgwood-Benn, Big Ben, Miss Gwyneth Dogoody, Tony Benn, Ben Stansgate, Stan Bensgate, Sir Raymond Gower and his son, David, Tony Stansgate, Ben Wedgwood, Neil Pillock, the Serjeant at Arms,

William Pitt the Younger, Arthur Bottomley, Tony Wedgwood-Bottomley, Anthony Wedgwood-Benn the Younger, the Duke of Wellington, the Duke of Wedgwood, David Lloyd-George, Anthony Lloyd-Benn, Hitler, Mussolini, ex-King Zog, ex-King Ben, Dr Horace King, Lord Devlin and his daughter, Bernadette, Lord Denning and his son, Peter, God, and his son, Anthony Wedgwood-Benn – Mr Ian Botham.

I sat back in my armchair, cuffed the cat once more round the earholes, and it was as though I was surrounded by a shimmering and radiant glow.

Only I in the whole of the world knew the secret of life.

It was all pretence.

There is no reality.

All is impersonation.

All is . . .

And then I was struck by a cruel and sickening icy sword thrust into the innermost depths of my vitals.

If life is pretence, if there is no reality, then who the devil is impersonating the lady wife?

With mounting horror and panic I looked at her.

Dear God, what I had long suspected was true.

For the past fifty years I had been having 'relations' with Mr Denis Compton.

—7—

Hard Times

Dear readers, these are indeed hard times for lovers of our dear 'summer game'.

There is no doubt that it is now facing the severest and profoundest threat it has ever been called upon to meet in its entire glorious and noble history.

It is quite literally having to fight for survival.

Consider some of the facts:

The world's reserves of pad whitener and stumpers' gloves are rapidly dwindling to the point of no return.

A series of seven calamitous summers have devastated the world crop of sweat bands and floppy-brimmed sun hats.

And, if the Arabs place any more restrictions on the

supply of linseed oil, God knows what the lady wife's loathsome spinster sister will use for soaking her dentures overnight.

We face, too, these days a crucial and frightening shortage of cricket 'craftsmen'.

There remain in this country today only two makers of musical jockstraps, and these are both well into their eighties and rapidly approaching infirmity and terminal drunkenness.

The Japanese have 'cornered the market' in bat mallets and abdominal protectors, and German success in the field of thigh pads and netting poles has completely destroyed a once thriving export industry in Keating New Town.

How sickening to see thousands of young men, the cream of our manhood, the joyous fruits of our loins, going out to bat dressed in Volkswagen disposable underpants and Toyota digital arch supports.

And what of the values long cherished by all devotees of our blessed 'summer game'?

In ruins.

In tatters.

Day by day the old virtues of fair play and sportsmanship, of manly courage and gracious chivalry are being massacred by boot-toting Australian fast bowlers, cheque book-waving entrepreneurs with inside-out faces and illicit midnight feasts with tuck boxes and 'fast' umpires in the radio commentary box at Trent Bridge.

How Dame Peter West must long for a return to his sequins and his surgical dancing pumps.

At times like this, dear readers, there are but two

comforts to console men of a cricketing bent – the church and the bottle.

Let us, therefore, crack open a bottle of our favourite Voce and Larwood finest dry Madeira, light up a pipeful of Captain Lock's rum-flavoured shag and seek the solace of the church.

Through what means shall we achieve this?

Simple.

Through the agency of the works of the Rev. A. K. Mole-Drably.

Readers of a previous book written by that verminous lout, Tinniswood, may recall a sermon I recounted, which had been given by Mole-Drably at the service designated in the Book of Common Prayer as 'the Third Sunday after the Lords Test'.

The text of that sermon was thus:

'And, behold, Ron Saggers did tour England with the 1948 Australians and, lo, not a single Test match did he play in.'

Many of you were kind enough to communicate with me by unstamped letter or reverse charge phone call to apprise me of the comfort this sermon had brought you.

'Bedwetter' of Basingstoke wrote as follows:

'I have these strange urges when I want to take off all my clothes during the second day of the Edgbaston Test and rub my body with dubbin and cloves cordial. Have you, by any chance, a signed photo of Mr Don Mosey in the nude?'

And from Castle Arlott a lady wrote:

'I cannot tell you how much I identified with Ron Saggers. In the past I had always felt a certain sympathy for the other 'Ron'. I refer, of course to Mr Ron

Hamence of South Australia. An illustrated booklet of the Australian Tour to England, 1948, in my possession describes Mr Hamence thus: 'Once set he is a very difficult man to shift.' How like my dear departed husband, the mobile librarian. However, on reading the Rev. Mole-Drably's inspiring sermon I repaired immediately to the aforesaid booklet and there read the following words relating to Mr Saggers: 'Given an opportunity is sure to please.' My late second husband, the piano tuner, was given the opportunity many many times and never once failed to please. Do you by any chance know the marital status of Mr Graham Roope and have you a signed picture of Mr Trevor Bailey in frogman's suit and lacrosse boots? Isn't cricket sexy?'

I confess that I have never looked on our dear 'summer game' in that light, although there have been occasions when watching the run up to the wicket of the immortal Mr D. V. P. Wright of Kent and England that I have experienced vague feelings of restlessness in the nether regions of the popping crease.

However, back to the Rev. Mole-Drably and the comfort to be gained from his sacerdotal ministrations.

You may recall that on the last occasion we encountered him he was the holder of the rectorship of the church of St Wilfred the Blessed Rhodes, in the county of Yorkshire.

No longer, I fear, no longer.

Poor soul, he it was who was the principal victim of what is now known to historians of the 'summer game' as the Yorkshire Schism of '81.

It is not for me to pass comment on the Jesuitical

casuistries and Mafia-like intrigues of the general synod of Yorkshire CCC.

These are far too complex and complicated for laymen to cope with and are only to be completely understood in the innermost recesses of the Vatican and the most sacred ministries of the *Daily Telegraph* sports department.

Suffice it to say that after the banishment of St John Hampshire to Derbyshire, Mole-Drably found himself in the impossible position of having to choose between the theory of divine omnipotence as proposed by St Raymond D'Illingworth or the 'Fitzwilliam Heresy' of Bishop Boycott.

Our friend chose to side with the latter, and thus found himself instantly deprived of his living with the swiftness of a Chris Old declaring himself unfit to play in a West Indies Test Match.

Times were indeed hard for him thereafter.

An unhappy period acting as baggage master and scorer for Mr Gerald Priestland was followed by a spell as part-time padre to the Wombwell Cricket Lovers' Society and personal confessor to Mr Cliff Richard.

At length, like most of the pathetically few Yorkshire heretics who have escaped being burned at the stake at Bramall Lane, flogged, hung, drawn and quartered at Bradford, stoned at Leeds and tarred and feathered at Scarborough (in that order of play), he sought sanctuary in the bleak and near inaccessible monasteries of the Derbyshire Orthodox Church.

That beloved, chaste and virtuous leader of the Church, His Blissful and Sublime Holiness the Archpatriarch Barry Wood, clasped him warmly in his arms, kissed him thrice upon the cheeks and uttered in his silken, mellifluous voice those ancient and moving words of welcome laid down by the prophets of his church so many centuries earlier:

'Hey up, shite face. All right?'

He was conducted by Brother Steele and Brother Taylor to a sparse but comfortable cell in the monastery of St Fred de Swarbrook high in the peaks above Tideswell.

As he dined off Rhodes in the hole, fricasee of wild Dawkes and Revilled kidneys washed down by liberal draughts of Harvey-Walkerbangers, the kindly old abbot and scholar, Father Cliffordus Gladwinius, read aloud to him from the works of Chaucer.

For Mole-Drably it was as though a great weight had been lifted from his mind as he listened to the abbot reciting those well-loved tales that have so charmed and comforted cricketers over the ages:

'Roger Knight's Tale.'

'Keith Miller's Tale.'

'Charlie Cook's Tale.'

'Vijay Merchant's Tale.'

And, of course:

'The Wife of Botham's Tale.'

For the first time in many months he slept soundly and as he awoke to the dawn chorus of peewit and pipit and the chanted devotions of aged medium-pacers, he resolved there and then that he would dedicate the whole of the rest of his life to the writing of sacred books.

I have in my possession now some of these works, and

they occupy a place of pride and prominence in my study at Witney Scrotum.

It is from one of these works, *A Treasury of Sermons for Distressed Cricketfolk*, that I present to you this most soothing of pieces:

A Sermon for Stumpers Stricken by Piles.
'And, lo, it is written in *Wisden* of 1981, page 202 under the heading "Four Wickets with Consecutive Balls" the following words:

'"S. N. Mohol . . . Board of Control President's XI versus Minister for Small Savings XI, Poona."

'I find great comfort in those words.

'You see, they mean, don't they, that however large a saver we are in the bank of life, or however small a saver we are, there is always the chance of being selected to play for God's XI.

'It might not be against the Board of Control President's XI at Poona.

'It could indeed be against Northants Seconds at Corby.

'But whatever the match at whatever the venue we know, don't we, that we will be awarded our "cap".

'As far as God is concerned, we are all in the running for representative honours – particularly if we can "do a bit" with the new ball.

'You see, wherever we may be, in Poona or in Perth, in Swansea or in Srinagar, in Brisbane or in Bath, we are being watched by the Infinite Being from his stool in the eternal long room bar.

'Whatever we may do, a "blob" at Sabina Park, a "hit wicket" at Amritsar, a decision to "dispense with bails" at Bangalore, an unprovoked attack of the Nawab of Pataudis at Madras, our actions are being noted in the books of the Immortal Twelve Apostles, chairman the Marchioness, Peter May.

'In whatever league we may "wield the willow" or caress "the crimson rambler", in Sheffield Shield or Currie Cup, in Ranji Trophy or Cornhill Test, we can be sure the Celestial Correspondent will send his report to *Wisden* and the *Daily Telegraph* and the word will prevail, and woe be to him who disputes that word.

'Who, you may ask, is S. N. Mohol?

'Who was stumper for Board of Control President's XI?

'Who was the Minister for Small Savings and did he give the four victims of S. N. Mohol a thorough good bollocking?

'Poor sinners all, we have no idea, have we?

'Our comfort must lie in the knowledge that when that great Umpire in the sky removes our bails at "stumps" and we are summoned to the great timeless Test of Immortality, all shall be revealed.

'I am often asked: Is there cricket after death?

'Yes.

'Oh yes.

'That I believe fervently, passionately, with a blinding faith as strong as the faith which maintains that the mouth of Mr Ritchie Benaud bears a remarkable re-semblance to a hamster's arsehole.

'There *is* cricket after death.

'In this we must believe.

'How else to explain the price of beer at Old Trafford and the state of the pork pies at Lords?

'How else to explain an innings by Mr Trevor Bailey?

'How else to explain the cricket reports of Mr Tony Lewis?

'There must be something more to life than that?

'Of course there is.

'There is death.

'And these are but the trials and tribulations we must all bear to prepare ourselves for the better life to come, when all earthly cares are lifted from our worthless bodies and our souls ascend to Heaven in a soaring, joyous upward curve like a mighty six from the noble blade of Mr Ian Botham.

'And when the heavenly senior citizen gatekeeper lets us through the turnstiles of the pearly gates, and we affix our eternal "wanderers" ticket to our purest silk John Edrich autograph shrouds, we shall find Paradise.

'And what is the Paradise, to which we all aspire?

'A cricket ground basked in autumnal sum.

'Shimmering oaks and copper beeches.

'Swallows skimming, bees droning and those noble words ringing high into the limpid air:

'"Will the owner of car FAA 811W kindly report to the secretary's tent. He's causing an obstruction outside the Taverner's Fruit-drop shop."

'And we shall recline in our deck chair, and we shall draw a mug of foaming ale to our lips and there before us in the eternal glow of our Timeless Test we shall see our heroes play.

'Jack Hobbs and W. G., Herbert Sutcliffe and Victor Trumper, E. A. McDonald and 'Tich' Freeman, J. B. Statham and Roy Tattersall, W. B. Roberts and Bob Berry, J. T. Ikin and Alan Wharton, Willie Watson and

J. G. Binks, E. H. Edrich and the blessed Winston Place.

'And we shall preen ourselves with pleasure, and the juices will flow sweet and languid in our veins, and, cricket being cricket, it will start to piss down and we'll get soaked right down to our vests.

'But let us not worry.

'That great Groundsman in the sky has secured his covers.

'There will be no leakages.

'And when the sun appears again, as appear it always will, there will be no "sticky dog" and play will be resumed on time.

'All will be peace and serenity as the Timeless Test progresses.

'There will be no lady streakers with things on their chests.

'The voice of John Arlott will be heard in the land once more.

'Beer will not be dispensed in plastic beakers.

'There will be no advertisements on the boundary fence for Pakistan Airlines or Toyota tractors.

'And when at close of play, we return to our homes, there will be no lady wives to rap our wrists as we attempt to change channels from "Hawai Five O" to "Test Match Special".

'And when we repair to our beds, we shall dream sweet dreams.

'Bowling out Don Bradman first ball.

'Thrashing Fred Trueman through the covers for four after four after four.

'Catching Vivian Richards for a duck on the far long on boundary.

'Being allowed to carry Ian Botham's cricket bag.

'Yes, yes, there is cricket after death.

'And those of you who dedicate your lives to God will play it eternally on those celestial pastures when your innings on earth is declared closed.

'For those of you who don't, it's everlasting rugby league.

'My next sermon will take as its text:

'"And, lo, Harry Halliday was a plump man, yet many a six did he smite for Yorkshire."'

I take great solace from these words, dear readers, don't you?

8
The Mole

I shall not prevaricate.

I know the name of the Mole in the MCC.

I am certain beyond the slightest shadow of doubt that I can reveal the identity of the person who 'tipped off' Burgess of Somerset, MacLean of South Africa and Alan 'Kim' Phebey of Kent.

His name is . . .

But wait.

Is it not better (to use the immortal words of Mr E. R. 'Elizabeth Regina' Dexter) 'to let sleeping dogs lie'?

The damage has already been done.

What possible good can come from the re-opening of old wounds?

And yet. . .

Yet when I think of the baseness of his behaviour, the vileness of his treachery and the voraciousness of his cupidity, my blood boils, my temples throb and the visor of my MCC sun cap hisses with steam.

Consider, dear readers, just a few of the evils perpetrated by this 'creature'.

For forty years, while occupying a position of deep trust with some of 'the highest in the land' he was actually selling to the Kremlin top secret, highly classified documents recording every single decision made by the English selectors over four decades.

What 'gold' for the Russian scum.

Just think of the implications.

The Russians actually knew before Mr E. W. 'Gloria' Swanton why Cliff Gladwin was dropped for the Fourth Test match against South Africa in 1947 and replaced by Harold Butler of Nottingham.

And it is certain that with the connivance of the Mole and KGB agents it was Russian influence which secured for Butler, when he retired from first class cricket, the position of Chancellor of the Exchequer, which, of course, to use more of Mr E. R. 'Elizabeth Regina' Dexter's noble prose, 'explains a lot'.

Worse is to follow.

With infiltration of this sort in operation can we be certain that the Russians were not, in fact, manipulating the decisions of the English selectors?

If this theory is accepted, it accounts for many of the inexplicable actions of the 'inner cabinet' which have occupied the minds of some of the world's greatest historians over the past century.

Why, for example, did Mr Tommy Greenhough play only four times for England?

Why was the great and saintly Winston Place never selected to play against Australia?

Why was Mr Alan Wharton not called upon to bowl in either of New Zealand's innings in the First Test match at Headingley in 1949, dropped for the next Test and subsequently never chosen to play for his country again?

A solution to this last question has baffled minds as great as that of the magnificent Mr J. M. 'Aubrey' Brearley.

But now we have the answer.

And it's a simple one – Russian agents were at work in the innermost vitals of the cricketing establishment.

And they were there through the efforts of one man and one man alone, whose name is. . .

No.

He is an old man.

He lives in peaceful retirement in the heart of our beautiful English countryside surrounded by his dogs and his books and cared for with love and affection by his two ex-Royal Navy 'spinster' friends.

Is it fair to them to rake through the ashes?

And yet. . .

Yet when I think of the enormity of his duplicity during the Second World War, I am consumed by a rage so violent it can only be assuaged by the swift application of my boot end to the rib cages of the lady wife's confounded Bedlington terriers.

Forget that loathsome bounder, Blunt, and his wife, Lyn Fontaine.

His treachery was a pale milk sop compared with that perpetrated by the Mole in the dark days of the last year of the war when the pavilion of our beloved Bramall Lane was used as a barrage balloon hangar, an adaptation which was to help Mr Fred Rumsey many years later while changing his underpants.

I can scarcely bring myself to describe the actions of the Mole.

But I must.

I owe it to my country.

So, gritting my teeth, flexing my upper lip and easing the elastic of my abdominal protector, I have to tell you, dear readers, that . . .

No.

Before I do, I must insist that you are seated, are of sound blood pressure and have within easy reach an extensive stock of strong drink.

These conditions are vital for your health and well-being, such is the enormity of the calumny I am now about to reveal.

Are you ready?

Here goes:

In the spring of 1944 the Mole actually passed on to agents of the German High Command in Berlin the blueprints of Gunn and Moore's new Charlie Barnett autograph cricket bat.

There.

The secret is out, and I feel relieved, for it has been a heavy burden to have borne alone for so long.

But is this the 'end of the affair'?

Can I in all conscience leave it at that?

Do I not have a bounden obligation to the land of my

birth and the members of the *Sunday Times* Insight team to reveal the traitor's name?

I feel I have.

So here goes. His name is. . .

No.

He is a sick man.

Publicity of this sort could kill him, of that I have not the slightest doubt.

Let us, therefore, draw a veil over the whole affair.

Let us content ourselves with revealing only the sketchiest and vaguest of details concerning the identity of this poor, misbegotten, misguided creature.

He was born at 4.37 a.m. on the morning of June 18th, 1903, in the small Lancashire village of Cardus-in-Tyldesleydale, which lies some five miles due east of the Trough of Bolus.

He attended the village school of St Cecil de Parkin, of which his father was headmaster and his mother chief groundsman and boilerman.

His academic prowess won him an open scholarship to Manchester Grammar School, which he attended from the years 1914 to 1921, when he 'went up' to Cambridge University to read political philosophy, classical Persian, difficult sums and the history of Derbyshire County Cricket Club, 1896 to 1919.

It was there that I first met him.

Now as I sit in my study at Witney Scrotum and see in the garden a flock of goldcrests and long-tailed tits quartering the conifers, a pair of bullfinches sullenly brooding in the apple tree and the lady wife perched high on the roof of the commodore's summer house, her blow lamp flaring, as she resolders the spurs back on to the weather cock, I think back to those distant and blissful days of honeyed youth.

It was indeed the 'golden age'.

Everything a civilized man could desire for the 'full life' flourished and prospered.

Draughty trams still rattled the narrow streets of cobbled Pennine towns, sailing barges still plied the muddied Broadland creeks, steam locomotives huffed and puffed up Lickey Bank, Cunarders fretted the waves at Mersey Bar, the blessed red rose of Lancashire was red and rampant.

It was the age of the sublime Harry Makepeace, the immaculate Ernest Tyldesley and the immortal E. A. McDonald and his opening bowling partner, Miss Nelson Eddy.

It was the age of O. S. Nock and the inimitable Robertson Glasgow and his dearly loved catch phrase; 'Oh, Calamity'.

There was not the slightest hint of impending Cliff Richards or Petunia Clark.

Life was gracious and elegant, and high society was bewitched and entranced by the beauty and wit of Lady Henry Cooper and Dame Peter West.

It was in this atmosphere of peace and serenity that I first met the Mole.

He was a 'correct' young man.

His togs were 'decent'.

His manner was diffident but friendly.

He had a firm handshake.

Dear God, I had no idea he was a bugger, a sodomite and a nancy boy to boot.

I confess I had my doubts about his chum, Nigel,

whose flowered shirt and crushed greengage-coloured velvet pantaloons made me suspect that he was not, as the Mole averred, the opening bowling partner of Mr Reg Perks of Worcestershire and England.

I felt, too, that Aubrey and Hector, despite the Mole's earnest protestations, were not members of the Leicestershire CCC ground staff with special responsibility for the maintenance of Mr L. G. Berry's toenails.

I suppose in those days I was an innocent.

I had not 'cottoned on'.

I sincerely believed that life was inherently nice, that the sun would never set on the British Empire, that the 'fairer sex' and all amateur county cricket players were totally lacking in pubic hair.

Imagine my shock on my first sight of Mr Kenneth Cranston 'in the buff'.

Imagine my mortification, too, on discovering that the Mole was (to use the delicate and sensitive prose of Mr E. R. 'Elizabeth Regina' Dexter) a 'raging poofta and a screaming bender'.

How could I have suspected it?

My friend's credentials were impeccable.

After coming down from Cambridge he passed his entrance examinations to MCC with 'flying colours'.

Within the year he was appointed chief of chancery of the MCC mission to the Vatican, where he became chief instructor in leg breaks and googlies to the Holy Father.

After only six months in that post he was elevated to the position of Chief Administrator (Cricket) MCC Antarctic Territories, where he was instrumental in developing the blubber-powered heavy roller for use in Old Trafford Test matches.

Thereafter his promotion was swift and spectacular:

1926–1931 *chef de cabinet* to Mr E. W. 'Gloria' Swanton at the *Daily Telegraph*.

1931–1933 League of Nations permanent delegate to Yorkshire County Cricket Club.

1933–1937 MCC ambassador to the court of King Zog of Albania where he introduced the printed score card and the tea interval.

1937–1939 private tutor to Mr H. D. 'Dicky' Bird.

It was then he achieved the ultimate accolade of being appointed to the MCC Museum at Lords as chief curator, jock straps.

We now know, however, that that was but 'a front'.

The Mole's real job was head of counter intelligence in MCC, the so-called, Cambridge-dominated Dewesieme Bureau.

It was the pinnacle of his career of treachery.

It was what his Russian masters had worked for all those years since they had suborned him in Cambridge by taking photographs of him of a compromising nature involving a cardboard cut-out model of Mr Leslie Saroney, a pair of Mr 'Patsy' Hendren's underpants and an inflatable rubber sightscreen.

He was a puppet to the strings pulled by the KGB.

Does that excuse his traitorous activities?

Who am I to say?

I am not God or Robin Marlar.

Certainly in all those years I knew him I had not the slightest reason to suspect the double role he was playing.

How was I to know that throughout the whole of the Second World War and the subsequent confrontations of the cold war he was supplying information to Russian and German alike?

When I visited him during the last war he always seemed such a normal chap as he sat in the madeira lace hammock on his lawn, idly tossing greengage pips at the doodlebugs chugging overhead and smiling with benign pleasure as he watched the tattoos rippling on the forearms of his two ex-Royal Navy 'spinster' friends as they knitted trench comforters in pink angora for the lads from the nearby ack ack battery.

The hock he served on those occasions was always exquisite and never once did I have cause to complain about the quality of his caviar.

And yet all the time the loathsome stinker was passing secrets to his masters in Moscow and Berlin.

What were those secrets?

I cannot be certain.

I am not God or Barry Took.

I am, however, convinced that it was he who passed on to the Russians the top-secret information that MCC would indeed open an Eastern Front by allowing Essex CCC to play first-class county cricket at Southend.

He it was, too, who was consistently passing highly-classified information to the Russians during the Great Powers crisis of 1950/51 which reached its culmination with the airlift of Tattersall to Australia.

Call me naive, if you will, but I suspected nothing when he quizzed me for information regarding the combination of the lock on Mr E. W. 'Gloria' Swanton's *Roget's Thesaurus*.

I took it as quite natural that he should show a keen interest in the latest opening batting experiments con-

ducted on the test beds at Lords by Mr Sam 'Werner
Von' Brown.

And I confess I found nothing to alarm me when he
asked:

'If Hitler were to conquer and occupy England, do
you think Yorkshire would allow Germans to play for
their county?'

I said I was convinced they would, as their committee
seemed to consist entirely at that time of members of the
Gestapo and close relatives of Hermann Goering.

Yes, I was a blind fool, I admit.

Even so, dear readers, charity and hindsight compel
me to confess that in my heart of hearts I am prepared to
forgive him for these treacheries.

And for what reason?

Because, dear readers, he claims that he did not as the
Sunday Times and Mr Chapman Snitcher would have
us believe give away secrets to this country's bitterest
and most unforgiving of enemies (I refer, of course, to
Australia) but was, in fact, working all the time as a
'double agent'.

I have no means of confirming this.

I have no means of disproving it.

I am not God or Roy Plomley.

All I can do is present for your judgment the 'facts' he
presented to me on the last occasion I visited him.

He claims that it was he who before the crucial final
Test match at the Oval in 1953 passed on to the
Australian skipper, Mr Lindsay Hassett, the informa-
tion – incorrect as we now know – that Mr G. A. R.
Lock had secretly become a deacon of the Church of
Fullers the Avenger, and would thus refuse to bowl in

Australia's second innings on religious grounds – or indeed any other grounds for that matter.

Did this false information completely alter the tactics of the minute, large-eared Australian skipper and so hand the match to England 'on a plate'?

Who can say?

I most certainly cannot, for I am not God or Clive James.

Incidentally, according to the Mole, Clive James is not all he is 'cracked up' to be.

He is, in fact, the reincarnation of Archie Andrews, although my friend steadfastly refuses to reveal who is working him.

I will not detain you with intricate details of his other revelations.

Suffice it for me to answer a few of the burning questions which these disclosures will raise in your minds.

Yes, it *was* Edgar Britt's riding boots.

No, Mr Keith Miller did not say that to Miss Iris Murdoch, although he might have said it to Edgar Britt.

No, Jan Morris is not the sister of Mr A. R. Morris.

Seven times, if we include the half-hour session in the curator's portable commode at Perth.

Dame Vera Lynn, Max Walker, Jean Rhys, Ian Chappell, Miss Margaret Drabble and her father, Phil, Keith Miller and Mr H. D. 'Dicky' Bird.

The *salon privé* at Edgbaston, July 12th, 1968.

Flatulence.

His wife would not allow him.

Seven and a half inches.

In Mr David Constant's panama hat.

How do I know? I am not God or O. S. Nock, although, by jingo, I wish I were the latter.

One vital question remains to be answered.

How did the Mole pass on this information to his masters?

By clandestine meetings in midnight gents urinals, by hollows in lonely wayside trees, by homing pigeon, by high-powered radio?

No.

It is simpler than that.

The information was passed through coded messages in *Wisden's Cricketers' Almanack*.

Yes, take another long draught of your strong liquor, dear readers, for it is indeed a terrible and most grievous shock I know.

But we must steel ourselves and face the truth with fortitude – our "bible" has been irretrievably dispoiled.

Who can ever read its noble prose again without a cringe of outrage, a sickening of the soul, a silent howl of despair?

And where does the key to the code lie?

In a simple passage in the *Almanack* of 1948 contained in the first paragraph of page 642.

I quote:

Abundant sunshine brought fresh vigour and zest into Scottish cricket in 1947, more interest than ever being taken in the game. Many English visitors seemed surprised to find cricket quite so well played and intelligently followed, and, on being told that as many as ten thousand people would watch a local 'Derby' such as Perthshire versus Forfarshire, their surprise was increased still further.

Dear God, it is too much to bear.

I will, I will, I will.

I will reveal the dastardly traitor's name.

It is. . .

No.

Let us give him a taste of his 'own medicine'.

You have the code, dear readers.

Work it out for yourselves.

His name is contained in this passage from page 942 of *Wisden's Almanack*, 1950:

A player or umpire will be paid the cost of a first class railway fare from the ground on which he was last engaged or from his home if he has not been immediately engaged prior to the Test Match. He will similarly be paid the cost of a first class railway fare to the ground on which he is next engaged or to his home if he is not so engaged. If a player or umpire travels by car he may claim the equivalent railway fare as stipulated above, but may not claim garage charges in addition.

No, God damn it, it is *not* Nancy Banks-Smith.

Try again.

9
Apartheid

Like all lovers of the 'summer game' I am appalled at the beastliness surrounding MCC's recent tour to India.

To quote the memorable and stunningly majestic words of the distinguished journalist, essayist, poet, philosopher and biographer of Mr Michael Parkinson, Mr E. R. 'Elizabeth Regina' Dexter:

'It's a rum old world we live in.'

I agree.

Indeed I am tempted to be even more provocative and at the risk of courting widespread public odium and being refused service in the village dog biscuit shop, state quite categorically and without reservation of any sort that I am all in favour of apartheid.

Before condemning me out of hand, dear readers, I beg of you to search deep into your hearts and your consciences.

Go on.

Admit it.

You know it's true.

They are not like us.

Scientists have proved conclusively that they are inferior beings in every respect.

They are inferior mentally.

They are inferior emotionally.

And while they may be stronger physically, their moral fibre is most certainly of the flimsiest nature.

Let us not beat about the bush – we find their appearance revolting, don't we?

And we know that their presence in civilized western society is totally disruptive and the cause of most of the major disasters that have afflicted us this century.

So why on earth do they want to live in our midst?

It is a proven fact of nature that basically and deep down they are at their happiest and their most harmless when they are 'amongst their own'.

So why should they be allowed to travel in the same trains as us, to drink at the same clubs, to live in the same neighbourhoods, and, horror of horror, be admitted to that bastion of all that is most noble and honourable and precious in this dear country of ours – the cricket pavilion?

Good God, they are women.

And we are men.

And, as far as I am concerned, 'ne'er the twain shall meet'.

The more observant amongst you, dear readers, will probably have noticed that there are certain differences of a physical nature between us.

'They' have certain appendages which we just do not have.

In this context I refer specifically to loud voices, hairy legs and sharp shins.

'They' have also what I can only describe as 'things' on the front of their chests, which play havoc with the shape of long-cherished cricket sweaters, which they insist on wearing when taking their confounded Bedlington terriers ratting in the coppice at Cowdrey's Bottom or mucking out the stables at their loathsome unmarried sister's establishment at . . .

No.

I must restrain myself.

With all the calmness and sweet reason I can muster I place my case before you simply and without embellishment of any sort – we are two totally separate races and it is against the law of nature that we should mix.

Look around, dear readers.

Consider all the happy and contented bachelors you know.

The Bedser twins, for example.

Can one possibly imagine the carnage and mayhem that would ensue if a bold, wild woman aflood with the reckless passion and the hot-blooded Latin sensuousness of a Keith Fletcher were to get her hands on them?

Disaster.

In an instant she would rip from their backs their immaculate, hand-tailored Subba Row grey worsted suits.

In a frenzy she would wrench from their feet their immaculate, hand-tailored British Home Stores black nylon socks.

And what would she place in their stead?

There is not the slightest shadow of a doubt that she would choose for the poor, gibbering wretches crushed-gooseberry PVC catsuits and purple velvet moon boots.

Now this type of togs is suitable enough for sartorial rebels like Mr E. W. 'Gloria' Swanton or Mr Donald Carr and his sister, Pearl, or Captain Mark Phillipson, son of the former distinguished Lancashire cricketer and umpire, Eddie.

But for the Bedser twins?

No.

Not at all.

They have no need of vestmental adornment to 'bring out' their natural gazelle-like gracefulness of form.

Like the pavilion at Lords, the outside toilets at the Garrick Club and the cardinals' sun lounge and sauna at the Vatican they should be kept completely free of women.

Consider their mischievous humour, their constant, bounding high spirits, their ever-sparkling eyes, the spring and lilt to their step, the twinkling animation of their voices – they are living proof that man without woman is a creature of nobility and towering strength.

When I think of women and the role they play in contemporary society (bus drivers, professional racing cyclists, members of Parliament of both sexes) I confess 'they've got me stumped'.

At the risk of appearing irreverent I have to state that I simply cannot understand what the Almighty was thinking of when he made them different from men.

I accept without reservation that it has been the making of ladies' netball.

But at what cost, I ask myself.

Consider the multifarious horrors this one act of divine madness has inflicted on us – mixed ballroom dancing, long fingernails, the ink monitor at Number Ten, knitting patterns, arguments, overlarge handbags, vile continental holidays during the week of the Scarborough Festival, confounded Bedlington terriers with pink bellies and fleas, loathsome spinster sisters incessantly sucking mint imperials.

I am aware that there are poor, misguided souls who maintain that women were created for the sole purpose of the propagation of the species.

Well, like all lovers of our dear 'summer game' I believe that that particular activity is a grossly overrated pastime.

There is far too much grunting and sharp toenails involved.

There are some so-called experts with their dandruff and ill-knitted Fair Isle pullovers who take great pains to inform us that the average man gets more exercise out of 'doing it' than he would out of playing a full match of rugby union football.

That may well be the case.

But I maintain that rugby union football is a damn sight more exciting and there are infinitely more tactics involved.

I am forced to the conclusion that the 'fly in the ointment' as regards the propagation of the species is the human reproduction system.

How much more satisfactory it would be if the lady wife were to lay an egg and sit on it for nine months until the wretched thing hatched out.

Dear readers, just think of all the advantages.

The lady wife would be confined to the house for nine solid months seated on her egg reading back numbers of *Pins and Needles*.

What possible excuse could she then have for accompanying you to the village pub at Witney Scrotum?

Ah yes, I know what she'd say.

'I could always stick the egg in the oven for a while,' she'd say in those familiar odious hectoring tones.

Absolute balderdash and tommyrot.

How could one rely on it with the state of the gas pressure these days?

It is patently obvious what would happen.

The oven would be switched on at regulo two. The egg would be placed inside. The man and his lady wife would stroll down to the village hostelry for two brief 'snorters' and a half an hour's nagging about the state of his underpants, and, when they returned home, the gas pressure would have gone up and they would discover that their son and heir has been turned into a Spanish omelette.

It just is not on.

I have explained the situation umpteen times to the lady wife, but still she insists on the statutory hanky-panky even at the height of winter during a commentary of England versus West Indies at Port of Spain.

Dear God, no wonder Bob Willis was no-balled seventeen times.

The whole trouble with women is that they will insist

on poking their long, over-powdered noses into affairs which by their very physical nature they simply cannot understand.

Take MCC tours to foreign parts, for example.

I am convinced that society as we know it in its pre-Petunia Clark heyday of Thermogene, Gillie Potter and wet battery wirelesses started to 'go to the dogs' as soon as the authorities allowed players' wives to accompany them on overseas tours.

How can 'our lads' concentrate on the matter in hand when they are being constantly harangued about the price of sprouts, the iniquitous behaviour of Nelson Gabriel in 'The Archers', the state of disorder of their sponge bags and the welfare of the confounded Bedlington terriers in their kennels at Langridge-on-Sea.

I don't give a damn about the welfare of the Bedlington terriers.

What possible concern of mine can it be that the lady wife has once again forgotten to cancel the papers?

Is it my fault that her loathsome spinster sister is unable to work the time clock on her central heating and. . .

No.

I must restrain myself.

I am a reasonable man, and I state publicly without prevarication that the institution of marriage has a great deal to recommend it.

It is only the presence of women in it which makes it so damnable.

I am prepared to 'go on record' and tell you, dear readers, that if it were not the custom for a man to marry a woman, I should without a moment's hesitation have plighted my troth to Mr Fred Rumsey.

Good God, at least he would have kept me warm in bed, and there is no doubt that his cooking would have been vastly superior to that of the lady wife.

Even now I shudder to the very core of my soul when I consider her culinary activities.

In the early days of our marriage I used to wait until she had left the room to fix the overflow of the lavatory, and then I would give the food she had prepared to our late-lamented Lancashire setter, Pollard.

Poor devil, it simply could not stand it.

One day it ran away, and it was three weeks before it was discovered attempting to tunnel its way into the free-range hamster farm at Keating New Town.

When I went round to the station pound to collect it, the poor brute threw back its head and howled.

It wagged its tail, it jumped up at my shoulders, and it looked at me with those great liquid brown pleading eyes.

I simply hadn't the heart to bring it home.

No, the whole problem with modern society is that marriage is being submerged by the vast amount of advice doled out by so-called experts.

What a ghastly shower.

What on earth was that pious and virginal Surrey and England batsman and slip fielder, Mr Grahame Roope, thinking of to allow his mother, Marjorie, to churn out such abominable claptrap each week in the *Daily Mirror* newspaper?

The much-respected New Zealand Test cricketer, Mr Geoffrey Rabone, has a great deal to answer for inflicting on us his odious mother, Anna.

And who could have imagined that that great polar explorer, Nansen, would one day torment us with his revolting, self-opinionated daughter, Esther?

The plain fact of the matter is that there is only one piece of advice which needs to be given to the younger generation when they are considering marriage.

It is this:

Never marry a beautiful woman.

If a man is foolhardy enough to marry a beautiful woman with a sweet disposition, his life is made an utter misery.

You see, dear readers, it is axiomatic that 'nice' people have always got more relations than people like us.

And what function do relations perform in the absurd hurly burly of life?

They place your home in a state of constant siege, borrowing the colander, frightening the budgerigar, using excessive amounts of toilet paper and showing interminable series of snapshots of their disgusting offspring winning fancydress competitions on P&O liners.

It is beyond dispute that the marital home should be a haven of despair and desolation, an oasis of rampant inhospitality. And, my friends, it is only a very ugly woman with a very ugly temper who will provide those conditions.

That is the only consolation I draw from the constant presence in my home of the lady wife.

In the early days of our married life her ugliness was such that on one occasion a close friend of mine, the curator of the golf ball museum in Witney Scrotum, was prompted to ask:

'Excuse me, but do you ever have "relations" with your wife?'

I answered:

'Yes.'

He responded:

'Why?'

'Simple,' I replied. 'I want to see what it is like "doing it" with a very ugly woman.'

'And what is it like "doing it" with a very ugly woman?' he asked.

'The same as "doing it" with a very beautiful woman, I imagine,' I replied. 'Slightly better than toothache. Not a patch on the Saturday of the Lords Test.'

I fear, however, that these observations of mine will fall on the deaf ears of the younger generation.

Poor fools, they are 'carried away' by the so-called romance and glamour of marriage – nights of passion in the boudoir, transparent negligees, dollops of talcum powder flung into the bottom of MCC bedsocks.

But in all this euphoria they ignore one crucial and fundamental fact about marriage as we know it – it involves sleeping with a woman.

And that is the ultimate punishment known to man.

What people simply do not realize is that as soon as a woman falls asleep she automatically doubles her body weight.

She closes her eyes, she begins to twitch and snore, she keels over on to you and – wop – it is like sleeping under the heavy roller at Trent Bridge.

Mind you, conditions are even worse when they stay awake.

'Do you know what time of the week it is?' they say.

With heavy heart and drooping spirit you reply:

'Yes. It's Friday night.'

'And what happens on Friday night?' they say, fiddling with your pyjama cord and making threatening forays with their thumbs in the nether regions of the popping crease.

'Oh crumbs. All right,' you say. 'But do you mind if I listen to "Today in Parliament"?'

That is the most unbearable ghastliness of 'the physical side' of marriage.

I tell you, dear readers, with all the seriousness I can muster, that if I had my way there would be a close season for it as there is in coarse fishing, and, if anyone were caught indulging in it out of season, they would be heavily fined and have their tackle confiscated.

And on that note I rest my case in support of apartheid.

Long may it flourish.

Long may the sexes remain strictly segregated.

And, if they do have to meet for the propagation of the species, it must be done under licence on the strict understanding that it is done for one purpose and one purpose alone – the finding of a successor to Sir Geoffrey Boycott as opening batsman for England.

10
Blofeld Revisited

The sounds of night deep in the English countryside at
Witney Scrotum.

Our batty, splay-foot bard and spinner, Undermilk-
wood, warbles at the moon:

'It is spring moonless night, starless and Cordle black,
and the hunched woollers' and watkins' wood limps
invisible down to. . .'

And at that moment an upstairs window rasps open
in the cottage of the village blacksmith, Gooch, and our
bard takes refuge as he is peppered with a barrage of
composition cricket balls, wicket mallets and the dis-
carded parings of Mr Ian Botham's big toenails (lethal
up to 100 yards).

Now there is silence.

Peace.

Then we hear the sly, snuffling feet of the village poacher, Prodger, as he slinks through the darkness towards his traps in the copse at Cowdrey's Bottom.

Owls hoot. Starlings scutter in the eaves. Wild geese cry.

And beside me in the conjugal bed lies the sleeping form of the lady wife, seam up, and a brief smile flickers over those familiar odious, revolting features as we indulge in a spot of mutual tummy rumbling.

I am content.

Memories of a programme on the moving television screen seen earlier in the evening glow in my mind langorously and sensuously.

Brideshead Revisited – what a magnificent story.

The corruption of youth, the decay of innocence, the blighting of high ideals – poor, poor Sebastian Coe.

A tear crinkles the corner of my eye, for I have a similar tale to tell.

It starts many many years ago in the honeyed haze of blissful youth.

But through the haze it stands out clear and sharp.

I see it now.

Still do I recall the poignant pain of my first sight of Blofeld Castle.

We had driven there, Lord Henry Blofeld and I, from Oxford in a friend's Hispano-Pilling open tourer.

The country lanes were warbled and leafy and beside us on the front seat sat Lord Henry's teddy bear, Marloysius.

'Take care he doesn't lose his temper,' said my friend.

And then as the sun mounted high we turned without warning into a cart track and stopped.

And there on a sheep-cropped knoll under a clump of elms we ate strawberries and drank a noble Château Prideaux and smoked fat and languid Ibadulla Turkish cigarettes.

We drove on for another hour or so and then in the early afternoon came to our destination.

Blofeld Castle — what a sight to behold.

A soaring, extravagant, sumptuous folly of broad windows, golden cupolas, plunging buttresses and flaring balconies, which provoked in me a near mystic trance such as I had experienced on my first sight of the pavilion at Bramall Lane.

'It's where my family live,' said Lord Henry.

And even then, rapt in the vision, I felt momentarily an ominous chill at the words he used.

We sat in the car for a while outside the gates, and he told me in a brooding monotone something of the history of that sublime and eccentric edifice.

It had been built by an ancestor, the rake and dandy, Lord Gower Blofeld.

Lord Gower, known to his friends as 'Lulu' because of his extremely short stature, his exceptionally foul singing voice and his remarkable facial resemblance to Wedekind's grandmother, had been deeply impressed by the riotous and debauched weekends he had spent at Fonthill and Medmenham Abey in the company of the Hellfire Club and its founder, the awesomely notorious Sir Francis Keating.

'Stap me,' he once said. 'They were damn near as licentious and bibacious as a night out in Herne Hill with the Bedser brothers, Alec and Eric.'

Accordingly he determined to take the staid old dank Norman pile of Blofeld Castle and transform it into an exotic fairyland of dark delights and coal black, slow black, crow black wickedness.

He spared no expense on his enterprise.

The finest craftsmen in the land were engaged to take copies of the infamous erotic murals on the BBC commentary box urinals at Trent Bridge.

Master masons were employed to carve representations of the hideously, monstrously contorted faces of the gargoyles on the roof of the Headingley pavilion, depicting incidents at a Yorkshire County Cricket Club annual general meeting.

Great painters were hired to transcribe to the galleries of Blofeld Castle the world's most celebrated salacious masterpieces, including Monet's 'Two Haystacks', a twin portrait of Derek Randall and Alastair Hignell, Gauguin's 'Why Are You Angry?', a delicate and subtly risqué painting of the confrontation between Mr Javed Miandad and Mr Dennis Lillee, and Toulouse-Lautrec's wondrous 'Leicestershire CCC shower room with reclining Ken Higgs'.

At length it was completed, but Lord Gower was not alive to see the masterpiece on which he had lavished his whole fortune.

Prolonged exposure to the cricket reports of Mr Tony Lewis and an unfortunate encounter with an infected cricket bat at the Cheltenham Festival brought him to an early grave and when he died in the arms of his beloved companion, Sir Francis Keating, his last words were:

'When you write my obituary in the Guardian, for Gd's ake mke sure yous pell my nome tight.'

When my friend, Lord Henry, had finished his story, he turned to me suddenly and said savagely through clenched teeth:

'Cricket!'

And once more I felt an icy chill dig deep into my vitals.

But for the moment I was enchanted and bewitched as we drove round the front of the house into a side court and entered through the fortress-like, stone-vaulted passages of the servants' quarters.

'I want you to meet Nanny Grimmett,' said Lord Henry. 'That's what we've come for.'

We pushed open the door of her room, and the old lady turned and said:

'Well, this is a surprise.'

Lord Henry kissed her, but before I had time to take stock of my surroundings she had padded me up, handed me a Gunn and Moore three-springer and given me a strenuous half-hour in the nets.

The fingers were rheumy, the limbs were stiff, but, by God, the old lady could still bowl a damnable googly.

I had to use all my wiles to keep my castle intact.

Lord Henry lounged on a chaise longue and watched the proceedings sulkily.

'Your friend has an excellent lofted on drive,' said Nanny Grimmett. 'Although I fear his stance is too square on to deal effectively with over-pitched seamers on the off stump.'

'Cricket,' said Lord Henry viciously.

Then he sighed long and hard and, taking me by the arm, said:

'Come on. I suppose we had better meet my family.'

It was as we descended the narrow stairs that led from the servants' quarters to the main body of the house and stepped into the main hall and paused awhile that I realized what had been haunting me from the moment I had first entered the confines of Blofeld Castle.

It was everywhere, an overpowering presence, a burning faith that could not be suppressed by decree or by dungeon, by gallows or by axeman's block.

It was an atavistic yearning that coiled and writhed deep in the souls of this ancient and noble family.

It was the faith that defies logic and flourishes riotously and rampantly on blind acceptance of its essential goodness.

It was, of course, cricket.

And its influence was everywhere.

We walked along the corridors and flanking us in rows and rows of glass cases were the exhibits in the world's finest, most comprehensive collection of cricket erotica.

I stopped, bewitched and enchanted, before a case containing the photographs of Mr Patrick Eagar, entitled 'The Nude in County Cricket'.

I saw a hand-tooled copy of the rare first edition of Mr E. W. 'Gloria' Swanton's *A Down and Out in Hove and Tonbridge Wells*.

I gasped in awe at the lead sphere immersed in sterile water embedded in six feet of pre-stressed concrete, which contained a lock of Mr Ian Chappell's pubic hair.

And there next to that was, naughtiness of naughtiness, Mr Fred Rumsey's left sock.

Lord Henry suddenly stopped, opened a door and pushed me inside.

'I suppose you want to see this,' he said.

It took me a few seconds for my eyes to adjust to the light, but when I took in the scene that presented itself to me, I gasped.

We were in a long and narrow room decorated in the arts and crafts style of the last century.

Angels in printed cotton smocks, rambler roses, flower-spangled meadows, frisking lambs, texts in Celtic scripts, saints in armour covered the walls in an intricate pattern of clear, bright colours.

'What is it?' I said.

'It's the indoor batting school,' said Lord Henry.

'Golly,' I said.

'It was Papa's wedding present to Mama,' said my friend.

We left the room in silence.

Many years later I was to repaint its walls with scenes in the life of Winston Place, including 'The Late Cutting of D.V.P. Wright'.

Later that evening over dinner I was to meet the rest of the Blofeld family.

Lord Henry's mother, the Duchess, greeted us warmly.

'Do tell us all the news,' she said. 'Is dear "Tich" Freeman still tweaking the crimson rambler? Is "Patsy" Hendren still wearing his divinely silly hats?'

As we tucked into the plovers' eggs and the quail's toenails Lord Henry's youngest sister, Cordelia, clapped her hands and burbled excitedly:

'I must know. Will Harold Gimblett ever play for England? Oh, do say he will, Henry.'

And all the while the heavy features of Lord Henry's eldest brother, Birdy, were fixed on me in a morass of lumbering puzzlement under the peak of the flat white cap which he wore constantly both indoors and out, giving him an appearance as attractive as a condemned cooling tower.

At length he spoke.

'I am deeply puzzled,' he said. 'It is the laws of the game. Take law 20 – Lost Ball. I quote:

'"If a ball in play cannot be found any fieldsman may call Lost Ball when 6 runs shall be added to the score: but if more than 6 runs have been run before Lost Ball is called, as many runs as have been completed shall be scored. The run in progress shall count provided that the batsmen have crossed at the instant of the call Lost Ball."'

He shook his head slowly.

'Lost Ball?' he said. 'How can a ball ever be deemed Lost, if one acknowledges the existence of an all powerful omniscient God?'

'Oh crumbs, Birdy, don't be such an old Jesuit,' said Cordelia. 'It's the way the game's played that's important. The rules don't matter a fig.'

'They do to me,' said Birdy gloomily.

We repaired to the drawing room and there the Duchess read to us.

She had a beautiful voice and great humour of expression.

She read part of *The Lyfe and Good Deedes of Brian*

Bolus by the Blessed St John Stevas and extracts from *Biggles Plays for Worcestershire*.

It was a day I was to remember all my life, even though it ended on a note of enigma and bitterness.

As we sat smoking in Lord Henry's bedroom late into the night, my friend turned to me and said with a venom I had not suspected existed in his gentle and sensitive soul:

'My God, how I hate cricket.'

And then he smiled wanly and said:

'And so does papa. That is his one saving grace.'

Papa!

The fourteenth Duke of Wisden!

What a man!

What a tragedy, for in him resided the malodorous roots of the cancer which finally sucked the lifeblood from his family.

I was soon to discover exactly why.

It was Lord Henry Blofeld's custom to travel abroad during the months of winter.

Although there was no need for him to do so financially, he was in the habit for the good of his soul to fill in his time in foreign climes by writing abstruse and recondite articles for the *Manchester Guardian* and the *Sunday Express*.

So it was one late autumn evening he said to me as we lay nude on the roof of the nursery idly filling in order forms for greenhouses and garden sheds in the *Radio Times*:

'Come with me to Venice. I need someone to hold my india rubber.'

I jumped at the opportunity.

'We shall visit papa,' said Lord Henry. 'You'll adore him, I promise.'

I remember very little of the train journey to Venice, for during most of the journey I was incarcerated in the ablutions offices laid low by a violent attack of the dreaded Nawab of Pataudis.

We arrived at Venice in the early morning and were conducted by gondola to the Duke of Wisden's residence, the Palazzio Dexter.

The Duke greeted me with courtesy and an amused gravity of mien. His son he kissed full on the lips, and I remember feeling embarrassment, for in my family the only living creature my father ever kissed was his bald and toothless border terrier, Cotton.

My embarrassment was increased some time later, when, having dressed for dinner, I encountered in the drawing room a woman of quivering glamour and deep, sensuous mystery.

The Duke of Wisden introduced me to her quite baldly:

'This is my mistress, Mrs Lane. You must call her Carla.'

She smiled at me and touched me lightly on the knee.

In an instant my stomach was churned to butterflies, and I knew that if she had ordered me to do so, I should have agreed to fly solo round the world on the back of a one-winged Liver bird.

I recall not one thing of dinner, for I was overpowered by the grandeur and dignity of the Duke of Wisden and overwhelmed by the beauty of his mistress, Mrs Lane.

I could scarcely wait to change into my dressing gown

and wrench from Lord Henry, as we sat on his balcony overlooking the silken dusk shrouding the Grand Canal in her flimsy shifts of rose and violet, every detail of his father's 'past'.

My friend was genuinely surprised about my ignorance and launched with vigour into the story of his father's 'disgrace'.

This in a nutshell is what he told me:

The Duke of Wisden was the central figure in the great abdication crisis of 1922.

It appears that one of the grand hereditary titles of state granted to the Wisden family was the presidency of the MCC.

On the death of his father in 1922 the Duke of Wisden should have acceded to that exalted office, but for two crucial impediments – one, he loathed and despised cricket, and, two, he had fallen in love with a divorced lady, who, worse still, was American and, chagrin of chagrin, was a lover of baseball.

The Duke's lack of knowledge of and sympathy with cricket could have been circumvented for, after all, so many administrators of our 'summer game' have set a firm precedent on that matter.

The presence of Mrs Lane, however, and the Duke of Wisden's firm refusal to terminate his relationship with her, was an insuperable obstacle.

The 'highest in the land' pleaded with him to change his mind.

The King went down on bended knees.

The Archbishop of Canterbury preached impassioned sermons in pulpits the length and breadth of the country.

Questions were asked of Mr Robin Day and Sir David Jacobs.

The Prime Minister even went so far as to present a list of suitable candidates whom the government would be prepared to accept as his mistress.

'No, no, no,' bellowed the Duke of Wisden. 'Never, never shall I share my bed with Mr K. D. "Slasher" MacKay of Queensland and Australia.'

The result was inevitable – the abdication of 1922 and the Duke's banishment in disgrace from the land of his birth.

'So there you have it, my dear,' said Lord Henry.

'Golly,' I said.

Two days later I was summoned back to London to embark upon a career of service to King and country which was to take me to some of the most outlandish parts of our blessed and noble Empire.

It was the last I was to see of my friend, for in the early years of the 1960s I learned that he had met his end violently during the mass outbreak of bed-wetting among Australian fast bowlers and putative critics of the moving television screen.

Some say he was kicked to death by the first change seamer of Queensland.

Some say he drank himself to death on linseed oil in Melbourne.

I myself prefer the theory that he was bored to death by Mr Clive James in Sydney.

As for the Duke, I last met him under the most curious of circumstances.

I chanced to be passing by Blofeld Castle on my way in the trusty Lanchester to Cardiff, where the lady wife was in the habit of taking boxing lessons from Mr Joe Erkskine.

On an impulse I decided to 'call in'.

I was met by a scene of grief and desolation.

Cordelia it was who told me that three weeks previously the Duke of Wisden had arrived totally unexpectedly at Blofeld Castle and announced to his family that he had come home to die.

He had repaired immediately to the great state bedroom with its bas-reliefs of the laying down of the covers at Bramall Lane, its ornate baroque ceiling adrift with nymphs and cherubs, seraphs and Gloucester stumpers, its golden statuettes of St Christopher Martin-Jenkins, and there he lay, placid and content to await his death.

'It's a damn nuisance really,' said Birdy. 'The Square's crying out for its first cut of the season, and we just can't get the gang mower out from under his bed.'

'No, no, no, it's far worse than that,' cried Cordelia. 'Papa is so close to death, and yet still he will not repent. Still he will not allow himself to be converted to cricket.'

I shook my head solemnly.

I asked to be allowed to see him as he lay on his death bed.

'I don't see why not,' said Birdy. 'Everyone else seems to be there.'

Indeed they were.

Standing in silent clusters round his bed were the friends in 'high places' summoned by the Duchess in a fruitless effort to obtain the death-bed conversion.

I saw the Archbishop of Canterbury, Dr Gerald Priestland, the Moderator of the Free Church of Lancashire, the Rev. Donald Mosey, the Roman Catholic Bishop of Lords, the Very Rev. Dom Brian Johnston and the Archbishop of Wales and Pebble Mill, Dr Tony Lewis.

The Duke's eyes were closed when I entered the room, but as I approached the bed, they opened, and he extended his arms towards me.

'Go to him, I beg of you,' whispered the Duchess. 'He has been in the deepest of trances this past five days. It is as though he had been watching an opening partnership by Sir Geoffrey Boycott and Mr Christopher Tavare.'

I moved closer to his bed.

The congregation was still and silent as I leaned towards him.

His voice was weak and cracked, but within its soul I detected a burning spirit that would not be assuaged.

'I have been to the other side,' he said. 'I have seen paradise.'

Silence.

The clock ticked.

The Rev. Mosey and Dom Brian Johnston changed places in the commentary box.

The Duchess nodded to me urgently.

I spoke softly.

'And what was it like?'

A great and beautific smile spread over his careworn but still handsome features.

He spoke.

'I think it's going to be a sticky dog,' he said.

And then his eyes closed, his breathing stopped and his stumps were finally drawn by the celestial Umpire in the heavens.

The rejoicing of his family and his friends was staggering to behold.

They wept.

They sang.

They prayed.

They danced.

At last he had been 'converted'.

I slipped out quietly.

And as I drove down the long driveway I stopped the car and turned my eyes for the last time towards Blofeld Castle.

I saw Nanny Grimmett supervising a session in the nets.

I saw Birdy driving the gang mower in great swathes up and down the square waving wildly his flat white cap.

And I am pretty certain, although, of course, I cannot be sure, that I saw rising towards the heavens the soul of the Duke of Wisden.

It was conveyed in a cricket bag.

And on its side, written in letters of shimmering gold, were the following words:

'Sponsored by Nat West Bank Ltd.'

11
Cricket Ahoy

It is my firm and unshakeable belief that for lovers of our dear and blessed 'summer game' cruising by ocean liner could be made tolerable by one simple change in operations.

It is this:

The vessel should remain firmly at anchor in its home port for the whole duration of the voyage.

What the wallahs at cruising HQ wilfully fail to recognize is that it is totally unnecessary to entertain the voyagers with visits to loathsome foreign countries, swarming with greasy wops, foul-smelling Greeks, sex-crazed Spaniards and lascivious, free-loading travel writers for the *Sunday Times*.

What sane, right-thinking, civilized man could possibly feel the need for lectures by pansy flower arrangers and cabaret turns by Cardew Robertson and female go-go dancers with bad breath and fat ankles?

Good God, within a handy radius of the port of Southampton there are at least six first-class county cricket grounds.

Why go to all the trouble and all the expense of 'carting' us off to foreign climes when all the entertainment a man of discernment needs is on his very doorstep?

It is quite clear to me, anyway, that the vast majority of passengers on a cruise liner are there against their will.

The most cursory examination of the wretches is enough to convince me that they have been press-ganged from the scummiest, waterfront flesh pots of the East End of London and the foullest pits of the industrial cities of the North.

I confess, dear readers, I feel sorry for them.

They have been shoved into ill-fitting dinner jackets and shapeless evening frocks which are quite obviously alien to their normal mode of dress.

Deprived of their natural daily diet of fish and chips and mentholated catarrh pastilles, they sit helplessly at the dinner table wondering which fork to use on their salmi of pheasant à la mode Harry Makepeace.

And for most of the time while the vessel is at sea they are depositing the contents of their stomachs in cascades of vomit, for which there can be no possible excuse – dear Lord, no one is compelling them to read the cricket reports of Mr Tony Lewis.

These gloomy and sombre reflections descend upon me as I think back to a cruise forced upon me by the lady wife in the late summer of last year.

Sheer, unadulterated misery and torture.

The only crumb of comfort was the fact that the lady wife's confounded Bedlington terriers were placed in kennels for the duration of the voyage and returned home in some distress have being bitten several times on their respective rumps by the proprietress of the establishment.

Obviously a woman of some refinement with a splendid pair of choppers to boot.

However, for the rest of the experience the only sobriquet I can offer is a quotation from the immortal prose of Mr E. R. 'Elizabeth Regina' Dexter – 'absolutely rotten'.

Even now I shudder with horror as I recall that fatal day when the lady wife 'trapped' me.

The morning had started with such promise.

The post brought the lady wife the intelligence that her loathsome spinster sister in Cheltenham would be unable to make her annual visit to us owing to her parrot's going down with avian bunions.

Even better things were to follow.

The lesser spotted woodpecker visited the lawn, the milkman with the noisy thumbs was extensively savaged by the commodore's geese, and the 'Freezer Special' was cancelled on the Jimmy Young Radio Show.

Freezer Special?

Dear oh dear, what on earth is the wireless coming to?

All one receives on it these days are the unctuous tones of Roy Plomley and constant interference from Mavis Nicholson.

It has never been the same for me since the blessed Wilfred Pickles was taken from us and translated to that great Haywood's factory in the sky.

None the less, I was content that morning as I watched the lady wife slapping vast quantities of greengage jam on her cowering slice of toast for all the world like a hairy Portsmouth matelot daubing his underpants with protective tallow.

Suddenly she looked up at me and spoke the following words:

'I am not going to Scarborough this year.'

Can you imagine the happiness which flooded over me?

Dear readers, what was in prospect?

A week entirely on my own in the most splendid watering place on the whole North Yorkshire coast.

A week entirely dedicated to cricket, snorters, and sleeping in my socks.

No lady wife criticizing the breakfast sausages and dragging me off to the theatre each evening to watch the completely unintelligible plays of that profound stinker, Alan Ayckman.

Why he couldn't stick to playing cricket for Sussex instead of writing plays about people eating pilchards in bed, I shall never know.

I am not a prejudiced man, but if I had my way I should take the whole vile band of Scarborough summer entertainers and compel them to sit through half an hour of Max Jaffa and when they came out screaming for mercy, I should mow them down with a gatling gun and drop their corpses off the top of Oliver's Mount, and, if any of them survived that, I should inflict upon them the ultimate of ultimate horrors – a quarter of an hour in the presence of the Krankies.

Where was I?

Ah yes, the breakfast table.

I looked up at the lady wife, and I smiled sweetly, and I said:

'What's that you said, my dear?'

She looked at me with those piggy little eyes of hers glinting and her face breaking into a grin like a crack on a Brisbane 'sticky dog'.

'I said, I am not going to Scarborough this year,' she said. 'And neither are you.'

'What?'

'Neither of us is going to Scarborough,' said the lady wife. 'I have booked a cruise instead.'

In vain did I plead with her.

For a whole week I hung round the entrance to the village school at Witney Scrotum during the annual attack of measles.

Not a single spot.

For three days I stood out in the garden in the rain totally nude except for souwester and MCC spats.

Not a single snuffle.

I feigned malaria, beri-beri, piles, rickets, trench fever, rinderpest, gapes, heaves, staggers, scurvy, hog cholera and a terminal attack of the dreaded Nawab of Pataudis.

All to no avail – the lady wife would not budge.

And thus did we find ourselves that fateful Friday

evening trudging up the gangplank of a vessel whose name I did not quite catch.

I had an immediate altercation as soon as I set foot on board when some shifty-eyed Lascar attempted to wrench my cricket bag from my grasp.

'Take your hands off,' I bellowed. 'Don't you realize that in that bag I carry all the articles essential to health and happiness for a voyage at sea? – the complete waterproof set of *Wisden's Almanack*, three packets of disposable abdominal protectors and a self-righting, inflatable smoker's compendium?'

Worse was to follow when I was damn near garrotted by streamers flung from the deck as we departed from Southampton.

I gave the offender, a gormless lout in lime-green moleskin trilby and maroon Bermuda shorts, a swift cuff round the earhole and repaired to the bar, where I spent the remainder of the evening reaming my pipe and glowering at the nancy boy waiters with their gold earrings and false suntans.

The following day was made faintly tolerable by the lady wife's being confined to quarters as we crossed the Bay of Biscay, and I was thus able to spill my kedgeree on my lap at leisure under the benign, brown-eyed gaze of the excellent Goanese waiter, who, incidentally, bore a marked resemblance to Mr Leo Brittan, although I found his accent infinitely easier to understand.

Two days out and what appeared to be a bright, shining shaft of light to send my spirits soaring was of an instant doused, and I was once more plunged into gloom and despair.

The circumstances were thus:

While taking my early morning stroll on deck I encountered a man dressed entirely from head to foot in white.

Good God, I thought to myself, civilization at last.

I approached him jauntily, slapped him on the back and said:

'Whatho. Typical of the trash who organize this cruise not to tell us they've arranged a cricket match. Playing the dagos when we get to Casablanca, are we?'

He looked at me silently for a moment.

And then he said:

'Sir, I am the captain.'

'Even better,' I said. 'My services are at your disposal. I am a moderately secure middle order batsman and I am no mean hand when it comes to tweaking the googly.'

A massive scowl came to his vile face.

'I am not the captain of a cricket team, sir,' he said. 'I am the captain of the ship.'

'In that case, my dear sir,' I replied, 'get back upstairs and start driving the bloody thing.'

With what misery I repaired to the bar.

Fond hopes dashed.

The cup of happiness snatched from my lips by the cruel hands of fate.

I was desolate.

My whisky tasted like sewing machine oil.

My cigar tasted like the end of the exhaust pipe on a Co-op coal cart.

The potato crisps tasted like damp raffle tickets.

And then I spotted him.

He was sitting on his own, surreptitiously appending

moustaches to the faces of the ladies on the mural entitled: 'Aphrodite and Handmaidens Fleeing from the Grasp of Alan Jones at Swansea – Glamorgan versus Worcestershire.'

It was a familiar face.

It was a very familiar face.

It was.

It wasn't.

It couldn't be.

By thunder, it was.

'Tufty Stackpole,' I bellowed at the top of my voice.

He started and spilled a tray of curried rice crispies down the front of his I Zingari dungarees.

A great smile of warmth and good humour came to his face.

'Good God,' he said. 'It's you.'

I pumped his hand and clasped his shoulders.

I had discovered a long lost friend.

I had not seen him for all of forty-three years when he had returned home from Burma 'in disgrace' after an incident involving a slip catching cradle, three members of the band of Troise and his Mandoliers and a portion of Sir Geoffrey Boycott's punkah.

'Tufty Stackpole,' I said warmly. 'By God, you've turned into the spitting image of Mary O'Hara. I hope your voice sounds better, though.'

Snorters were instantly ordered.

Snorters were instantly dispatched down gullets glowing with mutual friendships.

'Tufty Stackpole,' I said, smacking him on the thighs. 'What the devil are you doing on this loathsome cattle boat?'

He ordered a bottle of fine old vintage Brown and Robertson tawny port, and, as we sipped that noble liquid washed down with ice cold bottles of Umrigar's Fully Authorized and Harmonious Indian Exhibition Pale Ale, he told me the reason for his presence on the vessel.

He was to pay his annual visit to the cricketers' church at Casablanca.

'Cricketers' church, Tufty?' I said. 'What in the name of blitheration is a church like that doing in the heart of dago land?'

Tufty smiled and patting me softly on the knee said:

'I trust you will accompany me tomorrow when we dock, and there I will explain more fully the nature of my mission.'

'Rather, Tufty,' I said. 'Rather, old hoof.'

The strength of my good mood was further increased when the lady wife informed me over dinner that on the morrow she proposed to take a shore excursion by motor charabanc to visit the site of some ancient Berber burial chambers, the pictures of which looked remarkably like the gents urinals at Bradford Park Avenue.

'I don't suppose you want to come,' she said.

I said that under normal circumstances nothing would give me greater pleasure, but, owing to a slight attack of goat glanders and the threat of impending athlete's foot, I felt it would be unwise to venture into the interior without copious supplies of filtered water, oxygen, sulphur tablets and charcoal biscuits, which I was certain the vile dagos would be unable or unwilling to provide.

The lady wife arched her eyebrows and said nothing.

My mood of euphoria grew in intensity as the evening progressed and was not to be assuaged despite my being forced to attend a cabaret, which to my untutored eye seemed to consist entirely of arthritic jugglers and female singers with big ears.

After this odious event the lady wife marched me to the rear of the ship, where I was compelled to take part in a quiz game.

Why anyone should want to know the name of the capital of Nicaragua is totally beyond me.

And what possible good can come from knowing the identity of the longest suspension bridge in Europe and the author of Mrs Gaskell?

I apprised the quiz master of my views at some length and volunteered to take over the whole foul affair and conduct the quiz on matters of a serious nature – to wit, questions from my 1934 *Wisden's Almanack*.

The pomaded little nancy boy threatened to fetch the master-at-arms, a suggestion which prompted the lady wife to square up to the snivelling wretch and arch her eyebrows.

Calm was restored immediately.

I slept well that night and next morning went on deck as the liner entered harbour through clouds of powdered cement belching from some malodorous quayside factory, which seemed to me to typify the whole of the dago attitude to life.

The lady wife disembarked with her companions and enbussed on a motor charabanc driven by a rascally looking fellow with slant eyes and oily features, who bore a marked resemblance to Mr Leo Brittan, as indeed

I was later to discover did every citizen, male and female alike, of Casablanca.

Tufty and I waited until the activity on the quay had ceased and the hordes of dagos in Tommy Cooper fezes and Marks and Spencers nightshirts had departed to their stinking hovels.

We then strode down the gangplank, hailed a taxi and set forth towards our destination, which I was to find enchanting, enthralling and most deeply moving.

The cricketers' church of St Robin of the Blessed Marlars lies in a quiet backwater just off the main Muhammed V Square, Casablanca's equivalent to the square at our beloved Bramall Lane.

As we walked through the gate in the high stone wall and entered the rose-scented courtyard with its avenues of willows and oaks and its small immaculate lawns enclosed by miniature bushes of box and privet, tears sprang to my eyes.

Here in the very heart of dago land was a spot that was unmistakably, irrefutably English.

How moving.

How the cockles of my heart were warmed.

How my shins throbbed and my elbows quivered.

We did not speak, Tufty and I.

We walked along the cool, gravelled path, pausing from time to time to examine the inscriptions on the gravestones.

'A Yorkshire Professional – Washed Ashore – 1913.'

'D. J. K. Begby – Captain of Berkshire, 1878 – Died of Infections too Numerous to Mention.'

'L. R. Stopford – Died At Sea While en Route to Tour Sierra Leone with MCC – his Batting and Occasional Leg Spinners were Much Missed by All.'

And, most moving of all, in a sweet-scented glade, eleven simple white crosses with a plaque on a marble base bearing the inscription:

'An Unknown Touring English Cricket Party – Massacred by Riff Tribesmen, 1876 – Buried in Full Batting Order.'

With tears coursing down my eyes I was led by my chum into the church.

Here in the soft-flickering twilight he explained all.

The church had been established in the early years of the last century by MCC missionaries to give comfort and succour to cricketers en route to foreign climes and to pilgrims en route to worship at Lords.

Over the years it had been visited by famous and humble alike.

There carved on the reredos I saw the legend:

'D. R. Jardine Loves Gracie Fields.'

And there on the back of the second row of pews I saw carved:

'Bill Frindall can't count – Trevor Bailey.'

In silence we inspected the brass and mahogany memorials and then my chum led me to the innermost sanctuary and there he pointed to a stone memorial in the shape of three wickets with the off bail lying at their feet.

On it was written:

'In Memory of the Rev. H. H. "Foxy" Stackpole erstwhile Stumper and Cleric – Died of Whisky, 1911.'

Tufty lowered his head and I followed suit.

'My father,' he whispered.

And then in a hesitant voice, racked with emotion he told me 'the story'.

Long long ago his father had committed a mortal sin in the Church of MCC.

He had cast doubts upon the divine infallibity of Mr E. W. 'Gloria' Swanton.

He had been banished forthwith to Casablanca and there he had eked out his lonely years comforted only by loose women, the distant and faint commentaries of Mr Don Mosey and bottles of Glen Ranji whisky.

'My condolences, Tufty,' I said.

He shook his head.

He could not speak.

And then a most curious thing happened.

Stepping forward to the memorial, he pulled out the leg stump from its base, unscrewed its top and offered it to me.

'Go on,' he said. 'It's fully of whisky.'

'Whisky?' I said.

'My father's bequest,' said Tufty. 'I have been coming every year since 1932 to drink it. There's only a quarter of the leg stump left.'

And so in silence and comradeship we drank the last of Tufty's bequest.

Later, much later, in the evening we returned to the quayside only to discover that the ship had left without us.

I looked at Tufty.

Tufty looked at me.

'Come on,' he said. 'Let's finish off the off bail.'

We did.

How I got back for Scarborough in time for the last two days of the cricket week is another story.